How to make BIG Money in
Network Marketing

WIDE 'N DEEP

MULTI LEVEL MAGIC

Book Two – Shattering the Myths

AUDIO SERIES
Narrated by Alex Rehder

RON G HOLLAND
AUTHOR

OTHER TITLES BY RON G HOLLAND
Available in Kindle, Paperback & Audio

Wide 'N Deep #1 – Getting Started

Wide 'N Deep #3 - Building the Big Machine

Wide 'N Deep #4 - Click & Grow Rich

Talk & Grow Rich

Millionaire Secrets

Millionaire Mindset

Easy Ways to Make Extra Money

Information Overlord

Escape my Life and Live Free Forever

Insider Secrets of Raising Capital for Business

How to Earn Big Fat Fees from Niche Market Consultancy

www.RonGHolland.com

WIDE 'N DEEP
MULTI LEVEL MAGIC

Book Two – Shattering the Myths

© Ron G Holland 2015

ISBN-13: 978-1507645604

First Edition – January 2015

Ron G Holland asserts the moral right
to be identified as the author of this work

Millionaires Bookshelf
London - New York - Tokyo

www.RonGHolland.com

DEDICATION

This book is dedicated to Stephen Harris, otherwise known as 'The Amazing Hersky'. Stephen is not only the greatest magician that I have ever seen performing, but also the funniest and most generous man that I have ever met. It is a pleasure and privilege to be his business partner – working as a team in a great network.

And also to my beautiful and talented daughter Kay, who succeeds in creating magic every day of her life.

And most important of all, this book is dedicated to all our fellow MLMers across the globe, who are following their own dreams and aspirations…

WIDE 'N DEEP
MULTI LEVEL MAGIC

Shattering the Myths

CONTENTS

ONE: The 22 Immutable Laws of Network Marketing……..13

TWO: Shattering the Myths…………………………………...47

THREE: Forensically Examining Churn Rate……………...95

FOUR: Working in Depth……………………………………119

FIVE: Turbo Success – Reprogram Human Biocomputer….177

SIX: Isn't that Pyramid Selling?..191

PREFACE

Ron's Magic Incantation

Network Marketing, Multi-Level Marketing; it's fantastic, awesome, life-changing and wealth-creating. This is a business where you can really walk the beaches of the world and attain the lifestyle of your dreams. It is fantastic, tremendous, super, fabulous, amazing. Maybe you're after residual income, financial freedom, a pension fund, cash flow or business of your own. What turns you on? It's awesome, unbelievable, smashing and phenomenal. It is a business that allows you to work, when you want, where you want and with whom you want and it is something that you can do full-time, part-time or anytime. It is a business you can frequently develop in numerous countries around the world and it is a business that will afford you exotic cars, dream homes and vacations four or five times a year. What is your desire? Perhaps you want to be independently wealthy, leave a legacy to your family or increase your disposable income - Yes! Welcome to the incredible world of MLM, where, having some correct information can and will make the difference between stupendous success or dismal failure.

RON G HOLLAND

The Entrepreneurs' Entrepreneur

Ron G Holland is a seasoned entrepreneur with over 30-years' experience in the business mentoring, personal development, self-help and MLM industries, helping create 'True Wealth' and 'Growth Strategies' for the small Independent self-employed operator, through to businesses and organisations with up to $50m turnover.

Ron is a highly acclaimed author with more than 20 books published since 1977. Written up as: 'Leading Motivational Speaker', 'Top Biz Guru' 'The Jedi Master of Wealth Creation' and the 'Entrepreneurs' Entrepreneur', he is one of the world's leading exponents on the subject of thinking and non-thinking. Ron has given numerous business seminars and presentations and has been interviewed on TV, radio and press across four continents.

Ron's amazing business books, manuals and audio programs include *'Debt Free with Financial Kung Fu'* which was published in 1977 and has never been out of print and has been written up as, 'the most definitive book on getting out of debt ever written'. *'Talk & Grow Rich'* was first published in 1981 and was the very first book to introduce NLP (Neuro-Linguistic Programming) into the business and sales arena. *'Millionaire Mindset'* followed in 1993 and *'Millionaire Secrets – How to be a Millionaire in* 2009 - all of which can be found in institutions all over the world. Ron's amazing business books can be found on Kindle, Paperback and Audio.

Ron is a very special Business Guru and Mind Power Guru and over a thirty year period, Ron has helped many individuals become millionaires. Ron specialises in Personal and Business Mentoring and has raised millions in equity funding for early stage and start-up companies; creating new business opportunities and partnership deals. He also develops cost effective marketing programmes for small to medium sized businesses.

Email: TopBizGuru@hotmail.com
www.RonGHolland.com

FOREWORD

Why Multi Level Magic?
It's a good question and one that I am very happy to answer. For the past four decades I have concerned myself with success, creating wealth and high performance human behavior. Very early on in my quest, I discovered the magic of magic and have been interested in the subject ever since. Magic is analogous to network marketing in so far as when you watch a magician do his mind-blowing tricks and illusions, it all looks so incredibly easy, but when you try to do it yourself it usually proves to be difficult, if not completely impossible, of course, until you know how to do the trick. Obviously the magician knows all the trade secrets of what goes on behind the scenes which is usually hours and hours of mentoring, practice and rehearsal. It's this 'behind the scenes' stuff that I am going to share with you, so that you will have all the power tools at your fingertips, to build a large network, even if you do have to start from scratch. I firmly believe in MLM protocol and I also believe in full disclosure. I am at the top of a large and successful MLM organization with my business partner Stephen Harris who is, in his own right,

not only an incredible networker, but also a brilliant magician known as, 'The Amazing Hersky'. If you are in another network do not contact us, but use this information to help you focus on the job in hand, create magic of your own and make sure that everyone in your group gets a copy of this book or audio program for themselves. My contact details are at the beginning and end of this book and audio. Email me: **TopBizGuru@hotmail.com**

The main reason for writing a book series of books about MLM is that after thirty years' experience in the industry, is that I sincerely believe that there is still a dearth of high quality information, books, audios and in-depth training available to networkers, and that is holding the industry back - in a big way. The Wide 'N Deep series is my way of putting something back, and I hope that you enjoy reading and listening to them, as much as I enjoyed writing and narrating them. For updates on workshops, audios, books and big surprises, go to: **www.TurboSuccess.com** and download a FREE copy of Turbo Success to get on our mailing list. The definition of magic for our intents, purposes and analogy is as follows: Fascinating, captivating, charming, glamorous, magical, enchanting

PART ONE

THE 22 IMMUTABLE LAWS OF NETWORK MARKETING

Immutable: Not subject or susceptible to change
American Heritage Dictionary

Violate These 22 Laws at Your Own Peril
Ron G Holland

Law #1 Twenty percent of the people will do eighty percent of the work and sales

Law #2 Critical mass is necessary before any meaningful growth occurs

Law #3 All networkers are subject to the frailties of the human condition

Law #4 Not all marketing, compensation plans and products lines are created equal

Law #5 MLM is a highly regulated industry and those who flout the laws will suffer

Law #6 Overall company branding and positioning will impact the field

Law #7 You will never saturate the marketplace with a good product, only bad one

Law #8 If the products don't sell, no one earns a bean

Law #9 MLMs attract those who want to make money

Law #10 Prospects need to hear your marketing message a minimum of seven times

Law #11 Harness the Internet, modern technologies and communications or slip behind

Law #12 Effective meetings are the lifeblood of every successful network

Law #13 Strong relationships create sustainability

Law #14 It is imperative to teach and train that correct and meaningful things are duplicated

Law #15 Overall management of an MLM can either make or break a network

Law #16 If networkers are not locked IN, they will drop OUT

Law #17 The majority of leaders will come from the depth

Law #18 Organic progression of a network is always in depth - not width

Law #19 Large sustainable income will dictate that a large part of your network will be outside of your immediate payline

Law # 20 Working in depth is the ONE and ONLY tool that ensures MLM is a controllable business

Law #21 For every network there will always be an optimum way of building in the most strategic and sustainable way

Law #22 The one and only thing that really works in network marketing is the single, bold stroke

THE 22 IMMUTABLE LAWS OF NETWORK MARKETING

Before we shatter the myths of network marketing, we need to take an in-depth look at the immutable laws of MLM. These laws have evolved over six decades and have been ratified by hundreds of millions of hours of networking experience in the field by experienced pros, in a large range of diverse networks. These laws are not just extremely robust, they are in fact, immutable, and they are absolutely necessary if we are going to get past all the guff, hyperbole and general noise that we find within the MLM arena. Unfortunately, much of that noise is leading us further and further away from the truth, efficiency in networking and our own individual goals.

Law #1 Twenty percent of the people will do eighty percent of the work and sales

The Pareto Principle, which is also known as the 80-20 rule, states that for multiple reasons approximately 80% of the results will come from the effort of 20% of the causes. In 1906 Pareto observed that 80% of the land in Italy was owned by 20% of the population and 20% of the peapods in his garden delivered 80% of the peas, and many natural phenomena have been shown empirically to exhibit such a distribution too. In business, a common rule of thumb has emerged that 80% of your sales will come from 20% of your clients and certainly within network marketing, the 80-20 rule proves itself time and time again. You need to ensure that you are in the top 20%, leading, driving, building and deliberately causing results to happen and bearing this principle firmly in mind as you do so as it will assist you in your endeavors. The cream rises to the top, and this is replicated throughout life, in networking and in nature.

Law #2 A critical mass is necessary, before any meaningful growth begins

Critical mass is vitally important in networking; however, it is very common to see people quit before they attain it. Critical mass is the value of the parameter in which the set of equilibria abruptly change. In other words, you are trogging along like Wombat for weeks or months on end, trying hard to build your team and nothing exciting is happening. All of sudden you reach a critical mass, and then your network takes off like bat out of Hell, and you never look back. In many things in life, there is something commonly known as a tipping point and it is probably more noticeable in MLM than anywhere else, and I'll illustrate that here: I have used the parable before, but I'll use it again, showing the guy who gets offered a job with two pay options. He can have either $30,000 a month or $2 day, doubling every day in the month. Many folk accept £$30,000 a month, because at first blush, that looks like it could be a winner. It's hard to see how $2 a day, even doubling every day, could top that in just thirty days – but it does, by a long shot. Let's quickly do the exercise, up until the tipping point at least. So, the first day's pay is $2, next is $4, $8, $16, $36, $64, $128, $256, $512, $1024, $2048, $4096, $8192, $16,384 and you will quickly find out, that at the thirty day point, you reach $billion+ which is staggering. In network marketing, we usually maintain that a critical mass sufficient to invoke the tipping point is between ten and twenty people, providing each has been properly taught and trained to find one and teach one. If you manage to make this happen, you will have discovered the magic path to get into the big money in MLM, but also worth noting, is that many networkers quit before they acquire the skills to accomplish this.

Law #3 All networkers are subject to the frailties of the human condition and those with people skills will outperform those who don't

The principal resource of any network is the human beings that populate it, and all will be subject to many of the frailties of the human condition, both good and bad. This law is particularly worth bearing mind because it teaches us, that above everything, we need to hone our people skills as sharply as possible because every single day we will be colliding with all sorts of people, who are all patently very different. On the positive front you will be delighted with skills, attributes and emotions from people, including but not limited to: leadership, love, encouragement, hope, enthusiasm, positive thinking, sacrifice, helping others get what they want. People with these characteristics will enhance your life and help you grow, teach, train and mentor you and help drive your business forward. On the other hand you will come across an equal number of people who have negative attributes and emotions, including but not limited to: greed, laziness, naiveté, jealousy, overblown egos, stupidity, rivalry, arrogance, subconscious death wishes, impatience, petty mindedness, out of comfort zone. Inevitably you will meet those are convinced they are doing it right, despite flying directly in the face of immutable laws; and probably one reason for this, is that you can still make money in MLM even if you have done lots wrong – however, the Wide 'N Deep series is not just about making money, it's about making BIG money in MLM, and do to that you should work within the immutable laws, or suffer debilitating consequences, of which there are many. What I have learned about the 300 million folk in America and the 60 million people in the UK, is that they are all different. I have also learned for sure, that not all folk are teachable and trainable, but some are eminently more teachable and trainable than others. This business will test every cell in your cranium, every sinew throughout your body and it will test your tenacity; knowledge and use of psychology, wit, resolve, patience and closing skills. Harness this immutable law and you'll not only start making big money out of network marketing, really big money - what is more, you'll be a man my son!

Law #4 Not all marketing, compensation plans and products lines are created equal

Anywhere in business, where you have complicated formulas for paying out rewards and commissions based on percentages of sales, there is room for getting those figures wrong. Even slightly wrong may be enough to keep a company permanently grounded, so that it never breaks free of MLM gravity. Because of the large number of variables involved, not all MLM formulas will work and some will work better than others. History has proven time over, that if the company keeps changing the goal posts on the distributers in the field, by constantly altering the compensation plan, that is sure-fire formula for disaster, that not too many MLMs have ever recovered from. When considering joining an MLM there are many things worth looking out for and here are few of them: Don't join one where you have to build too wide because it demonstrates the companies lack of knowledge about what it is all about. Try to do some background research on the company and management team. A team of good managers with some MLM background and experience will give everything a good kick off. Are there already too many players in the market place with the similar type of product? It'll not be too difficult to find out who the other players are in the same sector – then compare notes. If the opportunity sounds too good to be true it probably is. If the money doesn't come through on time every single month, there is something inherently wrong.

Law #5 MLM is a highly regulated industry and those who flout the laws will suffer

In this industry it is very easy to find yourself on the wrong side of the law and be caught up in illegal pyramid or Ponzi schemes. No matter where in the world you are based, MLM schemes often get tarred with the same brush as pyramid selling or Ponzi schemes, and you'll notice that people frequently ask you, "Isn't that pyramid selling?" Over the decades, hundreds of MLMs have been shut down by the authorities for flouting the law, so you do have to be aware and enter business opportunities with your eyes wide open. Unfortunately the whole legal side of the MLM industry appears to operate in some very grey areas, so it is always best to hook up with companies that are using sound, professional and proven MLM lawyers. If you can join an MLM that is a member of the DSA, or one that intends to qualify as a member, that is an added bonus. When doing your due diligence, I would also caution that some of the worse scams have some the best, brightest and most plausible marketing collateral. This law is worth getting to grips with because there is nothing worse than working hard to create a residual income or a legacy for your family, if suddenly, through no fault of your own, the rug gets pulled from under you, the company closed down, and you have to start at square one. At the end of this book there is an Addendum entitled, 'Isn't that Pyramid Selling?' and this will give you some good guidance into the different MLM structures and the differences between illegal pyramid schemes and a legal MLM business opportunity.

Law #6 Overall company branding will impact the field
An MLM company that understands branding and positioning, is going to have a greater impact in field operations than one that doesn't. What is commonly misunderstood, is that how many things can be incorporated into the marketing, branding, positioning and packaging mix. For example: Does the website draw people in, tell them exactly what they need to know in order to proceed with the business proposition, and is ease of navigation all it could be? Are the sign-up forms too complicated or are they user

friendly? Is the money-back guarantee tenable and is it actionable immediately and without quibble? Is the marketing collateral sharp, colorful and written in plain English with not too many words on the page? Is the marketing collateral good enough to be a stand-alone silent salesman? Are the terms and conditions readily available and are they correct, legal and intelligible?

Law #7 You will never saturate the marketplace with a good product, only a bad one

Within MLM you frequently hear prospect being negative about an opportunity because they say it will saturate the marketplace too quickly. I can think of hundreds of blue-chip companies that have been trying to saturate their marketplace for decades, and none have come close to succeeding, despite having billion dollar budgets to help their quest.

Law #8 If the products don't sell, no one earns a bean

This is a powerful law, but it never ceases to amaze me the number of folk who still regularly proselytize, "No selling involved" and then leave all the selling to others. The hard reality is that nobody earns a bean, not the company or the distributors, if the products don't sell. When you consider the small amount of product that each distributer either sells or consumes on average in each network, it is very inefficient and usually a whole load more could be done to shift more product. There are three magic words when it comes to creating retail sales in MLM. The first word worthy of discussion is *'awareness'* and what I see is folk who are totally oblivious to the fact that the product needs to be sold. Start by buying more than the monthly quota, and encourage your network to do the same and seek out many more retail customers. It's worth thinking about, because ostensibly if everyone sold twice as much as they did, everyone one would earn twice the amount for the same number of people in the network. The reason why it needs to be done is that millions of man-hours are not utilized effectively, with each rep doing minimum sales. The second word worthy of discussion is that of *'urgency'* that products needs to be consumed by individual networkers and also sold outside the network to retail customers.

The third magic word is *'creativity'* and that is the key to shifting product in MLM. Get ultra-creative and get the whole family to get involved in sales drives and initiatives and make sure that the creativity and enthusiasm for creating sales rub off on the people in your team – then watch the products roll out the front door.

Law #9 MLMs attract those who want to make money, including those who are not suited to the opportunity

People who are attracted to business opportunities usually want to make money, but that doesn't necessarily make them suitable or competent for the job in hand. Whether it be an extra $200 a month to pay some bills, like it is for a large number of people or those who are more ambitious and want to become millionaires, but unfortunately not everyone is equipped sufficiently enough do to so. Many folk not only lack capital, but more importantly they may also lack the aptitude and mental resources to start a business of their own. This is an important law to heed, because often large numbers of man-hours are wasted in trying to teach and train slow starters; those not grasping the fundamentals or others with few people skills. Many cannot focus on the job in hand because they are frequently fighting fires on many fronts and this scenario doesn't necessarily bode well for them cranking up a storm with their new MLM business. Does this mean steer clear of anyone who has financial problems who wants to join your business? No, of course not, but it does mean that you should continually have your wits about you. Sometimes serious or experienced businessmen who have hit hard times or even bankruptcy may be just the animal that you are seeking as one of your leaders and your biz-opp maybe their savior and answer to their prayers. All the brilliant network marketers that I know, have the ability to think like their prospects and put themselves in the shoes of their prospects, and they do it over and over again. They also have empathy for people and intuitively know the difference between a wastrel and a serious businessman who is down on his luck.

Law #10 MLM prospects need to hear your message a minimum of seven times

It often amazes me that many who join MLMs don't fully comprehend the meaning of the words, 'Network Marketing' and believe me, the clues are in the words. The first word is screaming out and it says, 'Network'. Two things jump of the page, and that is 'net' and 'work'. You need to spread your 'net' as far and as wide as conceivably possible and you do this by continually building your prospect list. The word 'work' jumps off the page too, and I think that I mentioned before that unfortunately too many folk look at MLM biz-opps these day have unwittingly bought into the, 'no work required, no selling involved - all you have to do is pick up the checks'. In my personal experience, the people who make big bucks from MLM, and I know lots of them, work extremely hard and get paid handsomely over and above for what they do. If you ever see someone running down the road, laughing all the way to the bank, I'll bet my last dollar that it's an MLMer. The last word that I want to talk about is 'marketing' and in MLM that's what we get paid the really big bucks for. Any conventional marketing pro worth his salt will tell you all about marketing and how it works, and word-of-mouth marketing is no different. If I give you a potted history of how marketing works in conventional business, you may be able to turn that it on its head and use these techniques in your MLM - I hope so. Have you ever heard of Coca Cola; Pepsi, IBM, Microsoft, Honda, GM, Buick, Apple, Dell, Haagen Dazs, Mercedes, Ferrari, Virgin? Of course you have. When did you last hear of them? Today, no later than yesterday, I bet? What these big boys do is keep getting their message out there, in hundreds of different ways and they don't stop – it's Relentless, and I do mean Relentless with capital R. MLM Pros intuitively exploit Law #10 and they pitch over and over again and keep in touch with people over a long period of time and they too never stop promoting their message and telling their story - ever. Take a leaf out the big-boys book and do the same. Stop being naïve, thinking that if you told your story *once* to a prospect, and because they said, "NO", you think it's all over - but it just doesn't work like that!

Law #11 Harness the Internet, modern technologies and communications or slip behind

Technology can sneak up on you, and I do believe that we are already witnessing some MLMs leaving others in their wake, because of the intelligent and resourceful way they are embracing and harnessing it. Of course timing is everything, and some of the bigger companies lost hundreds of millions, by getting in too early, but I do believe the time is now ripe to start taking advantage of the internet and all of the technologies that go with it. The internet has made the world a very small place and it is all too easy to find your network taking off exponentially, in places you never even heard of. When this happens, droves of people are forced to use Skype, email and other mechanisms and devices that up until recently, conventional old-school MLMers shunned. I too am old school and was weaned on face-to-face meetings in hotels and conference halls and people's living rooms and coffee bars. Last century's methodologies have done us proud; but I can see things changing with my own eyes, at a phenomenal pace. I am fast becoming a fan of attraction marketing and find myself spending inordinate amounts of time indulging FaceBook, Google, Kindle books, Skype and harnessing twenty first century methodologies and technologies as fast as I can. Much of what I use, and plenty of what other pros use, I will cover in great detail in modules four, five and six of Wide 'N Deep and I promise that you will get as excited as I am – because it's digi-magical.

Law #12 Effective meetings are the lifeblood of every successful network

Although the type and location of the meetings may have changed, you cannot escape the fact that meetings are at the core of every successful network. It appears that these days more and more meetings are over Skype, FaceBook, cell phones and the Internet. But whatever the type of meeting, whether face-to-face or virtual, it is meetings that allow you to have the confrontation time that is needed to pitch, follow-up and follow-through and more importantly, 'seal the deal' with the prospect. If you can increase the number of meetings throughout your network, and focus on making those meetings more meaningful and effective, your network will grow accordingly.

Law #13 Strong relationships create sustainability

Although more and more is being done over the internet and through the use of modern communications, the truth is that more and more of the personal side of things is getting lost and that is not just a great shame, it could prove to be the death knell. The credo: 'Help enough others get what they want, and what you want is self-assured' is particularly true in MLM, because that is how it works and that is how we make big money. You develop strong relationships by stretching people, and constantly reminding them that, everything they want, is just outside their comfort zone. Encourage them to step outside of their comfort zone and when you keep challenging them in a positive way they will grow, and they will thank you for the support and guidance, and a strong relationship will develop. Being sensitive and giving the right advice at the right time is all part and parcel of developing strong relationships and sticking with people when they falter, until they regain their composure, is part of it too. MLM is the best factory and proving ground in the world for personal development and growing people.

Law #14 It is imperative to teach and train that correct and meaningful things are duplicated

Thousands of would-be network marketers trip up on this law every day, and maybe it's because they have never heard the expression, "What's the use of running, when you're on the wrong road?" I do believe Law #14 is one of the biggest magic secrets of all time and if you're not getting the correct things duplicated, it can turn out to be one of the biggest show stoppers of all time. One vitally important thing for you to take on board, is try to get as many of your team to understand and assimilate these laws as soon as possible. Unfortunately, within networking the 'monkey see - monkey do' syndrome is frequently the way things get replicated, be they right or wrong. If you're inadvertently passing on incorrect information, maybe through no fault of your own, this can dramatically slow down the growth of your network and the more distributors that take on board the mistakes, the slower growth becomes, until your network eventually begins to recede and ultimately grinds to an abrupt halt. Where I am leading is simple: This is all so important, at this moment in time I will just scratch the surface of what needs to be accomplished, and as the modules open up in later stages, we will explore all the laws, including this one, in great detail and leave no stone unturned, so that you may apply some real science, technology, psychology, and of course magic to your network. All of which will have the effect of getting you into the big money in network marketing. The salient point that really needs to be duplicated is quite simple: keep driving depth and stay in the leg that you are driving depth in, until you are properly duplicated. This may sound simple, but it is not easy, and that is why huge swathes of this book will be dedicated to getting to the heart of this law – which incidentally is immutable. We will take the guesswork out of what really has to be duplicated, and why so many myths are holding your network and our industry back.

Law #15 Overall management of an MLM can either make or break a network

This law states, that the more experienced and professional the team at the head of the MLM organization, the better it will be for networkers in the field. Younger teams may even consider engaging experienced non-executive directors and other professional advisers, and beefing up their board with older and more experienced talent. To operate in the increasingly competitive global arena, the team may need to broaden its horizons and think globally, whereby previously concentrating on North America would suffice. The internet and modern day communications force us to do this, whether we like it or not. Leadership at company level and field level is paramount. The management team need to both recognize and cultivate leadership in the field, after all, that is what is going to grow the company. They need to support the field in numerous ways; ensuring they have best possible marketing collateral at all times, ensuring the product range is timely, fresh, exciting and competitive, ensure the compensation plan actually works, motivates and drives the network, payments are made like clockwork on exactly the same day each month, and problems are resolved with minimum conflict and within the shortest space of time. It goes without saying that the compensation plan and T&Cs should be legal and above board and the company is compliant with State and any country laws that it operates in. The management team will also be aware that many hundreds of networks have disappeared over the years leaving not even a trace of bubbles and never allow themselves to become complacent, just because they own an incredible cash generative vehicle. Sometimes the Directors make the mistake of becoming too removed from the field and not getting a handle on what the sentiment in the field is really like. Other times I have seen the goal posts move so make times that distributors left en-masse for pastures new or set up their own MLM – sometimes, though not always, with great success. These days MLM is a highly competitive arena and if you don't get all the variables right, and get the network singing, humming and buzzing, distributers will still up and go – even if they are earning relatively good money. There is a lot that a management team can do to get ahead and keep ahead of the competition: Develop creative check lists of all the variables within their business that need kept on top of. Keep beefing up infrastructure, no matter how robust it is. Exponential growth does creep up on you, it suddenly overwhelms you. Form a mastermind group at company level and ensure there is mastermind group in the field giving vital intel back to the company, about what is happening on the ground. There are many competitors out there, so companies need to stretch themselves to be head and shoulders above the rest.

Law #16 If networkers are not locked IN, they will drop OUT

There are as many ways as there are galaxies in the universe for trying to achieve getting leaders on the front line and the technique that I have seen employed the most is to keep sponsoring personally on the front line and live in hope. I think the worst case I saw was a guy, 'Dim but Nice' who personally sponsored over forty people on his front line on the totally false premise that two or three of them would turn out to be leaders and run with it. Of course what happened, is what always happens, when you utilize the resource ineffectively and don't lock people in; they drop out, and to a man they did – all of them! By way of illustration only, I want you to draw a string of circles, all linked to each other in a vertical line, as opposed to the horizontal 'front line' those forty reps were placed. Here is the question I want you to ask yourself. In the first instance of forty people, all front line to our man 'Dim but Nice', how many people were locked in, excited and motivated and had a business that was growing? And scenario two, the guy 'Try Hard' who stacks those forty people in row vertically. How many people are locked in, excited, motivated and has a business that is growing? Well, in the first instance 'Nice but Dim' is the only one who is locked, in excited and motivated. Whether his business will grow remains to be seen – but it's doubtful. In example two, that is for illustrative purposes only, there are forty people locked in including 'Try Hard' who are excited and has a business that is growing. The only person who is not in that category is the last guy in the chain, because he has no one below him and therefore he is not locked in, excited or motivated or has a business that is growing. In relating this piece, I reminded me of the military story which I believe to be true, and that was the taking of Hamburger Hill, whereby wave after wave of troops were eviscerated through machine gun fire. The battle has gone down in history as the most infective and ill-conceived use of man power - ever. However, I am not sure if it is true, that ultimately a battalion of lawyers took Hamburger Hill - because they knew how to Charge! The only reason I throw this story in here, is because I want you to have constant reminder about the effective use of the only resource that every network has and depends upon – its human capital. Realize that just by getting someone placed strategically correctly, they are automatically doing a huge amount of work, even if they are not selling or sponsoring. Just the act of being there is working, and more often than not, is not even recognized – but it is priceless, and if you're missing this, you're not just missing PART of it, you're missing ALL of it.

Law #17 The majority of leaders will come from the depth

This Law is very much misunderstood, but in reality so simple and so obvious. This law works hand in glove with Law #1, that 20% of the people will do 80% of the work. This means, no matter hard you try, you will not get three leaders on your front line, but every day 1000's of network marketing entrepreneurs get it wrong, through no fault of their own. It is totally untenable and impossible to teach and train, although many try, and fail miserably. If everyone managed to get three leaders on their front line this would mean that the network would be full of leaders and this would be as impossible as it is ridiculous, and it completely violates Law #1. The best way to describe what any network looks like in real terms, would be to draw a triangle, say eight levels deep with three people on your front line and then nine people on the next level and then twenty seven people going right down to the eighth level where you would have say, six thousand people in the width. Now put on a blindfold and with a pin, point out where all the leaders may or may not be and that is what your network will look like, not just your network, but everyone's network, because that's how it works. Does this mean to say that you will never have a leader on your front line? Of course not, someone somewhere is going to have a leader or two on their front line, after all, leaders have to be somewhere. Does this mean to say, teaching and training doesn't work? Of course not, but does mean that you need to be teaching and training what works in harmony with how networking marketing actually works in the real world, and not violate any of its immutable laws. What it does mean however, if you understand this law and abide by it, you will work *smarter* and grow *quicker* and be *greatly* more efficient in what you do. The penalty for violating this simple law is many-fold including; slow growth, massive drop-out rate, continuous grow-recede-grow-recede, frustration and lack of profitability. A few points to ponder: You can't fill a network full of leaders so why even contemplate it? Why try to do something that even Mandrake the Magician couldn't do? Why teach and train that which cannot be replicated – ever. Sometimes it pays to draw out these concepts on paper, to help you visualize them and make them a reality in your mind's-eye. A little later on in this module we will explore in depth (excuse the pun) how to exploit this law to the Nth degree because if you can harness the law, you will find rapid growth, all the leaders you require, unrivalled retention rate and lock in rate, massive motivation, optimum profitability *and* sustainability.

Law #18 The organic progression of a network is always in depth - not width

In a way it is good that Law #18 exists, because it has the habit of keeping us on the straight and narrow with regards to how networks grow naturally, organically and easily. It is relatively easy to envisage that if you stopped building your network today, and came back to it in three years, it's true to say that your network will have probably grown in depth, but probably not in width on your front line. Growing in depth is the natural progression of things in network marketing, whereas as building width, although *sometimes* a necessary evil, is still working against the grain. If you build too wide, it's akin to keeping melons down in a bath of water; no sooner you push one down over here, two others pop up over there. Many networkers trying to build width have discovered it is harder to get one in through the front door, before two leave by the back door. You have seen how Law #16 insists that you lock people in and if violate that law, people will drop out. Once you have assimilated and harnessed this important law, you will be granted the keys to the MLMers magic circle – automatically.

Law #19 Large sustainable income will dictate that a large part of your network will be outside of your immediate pay-line

Of course it is easy to see, what leads network marketers down this booby trapped lane, and that is not starting at the point where you want to end up. Of course the novice to MLM or the ego driven networker is likely to say things like; keep everyone up close to you, whatever you do don't let go outside your pay-line, build for profit, why let the company have all the profit when you can have it all for yourself? Every time I hear these things, which is all too frequently, it tells me how little that person really understands the subtleties and sophistication of our industry. Coming up soon, you'll learn the real secrets behind this powerful, immutable law

Law # 20 Working in depth is the ONE and ONLY tool that ensures MLM is a controllable business

How often have you heard networkers, particularly when they are in decline or quitting their involvement in a network marketing opportunity, blaming everyone else for their dismal failure? They frequently use words along the lines of, "I got fed up with chasing folk, waiting on them and nobody would do anything. It was a nightmare. If they had all done the same as me, it would have been a different story, but nobody ran with it." When you work in depth, the last thing you have to do is rely on anyone in your network doing a single thing, until you have managed to teach and train a person to replicate you. Working in depth allows you to take charge, control and build your MLM business at your own pace. All you have to do is keep taking the initiative and work with people below you and don't stop. If you don't understand and assimilate this and it implications, you will be missing out on a huge part of what makes the MLM industry exciting, sustainable and attractive to serious business people. Suddenly it is not a game of chance, luck or having leaders on your front line. Working in depth ensures that can drive the business at you own pace and create the kind of momentum that favors growth. If you were not able to work in depth, you would be relying solely on the initiative of other people, and with Law #1 stating that 20% of the people will do 80% of the work, you would find it very tough to gain sufficient momentum, that is needed in order to create sustainable success.

Law #21 For every network there will always be an optimum way of building in the most strategic and sustainable way

Obviously all MLM businesses have their own uniqueness and these laws like all the principles in the Wide 'N Deep series, are designed to be generic information. What you need to do is take on board the immutable laws and see how you can combine them into a workable formula within your own MLM, as all structures are different, and not to take into account these differences would be foolhardy, to say the least. Remember the immutable nature of these laws, some things are impossible to avoid, like tightrope walkers say: Gravity never gives up!

Law #22 The one and only thing that really works in network marketing is the single, bold stroke

History teaches us that in conventional marketing, the one thing that works every time is the single bold stroke. Furthermore, in any given situation there is only one move that will produce substantial results. Network marketing is no different, and you will notice time over, that networks suddenly make a massive spurt in growth. This is because someone, usually a leader in the depth, has activated Law #22: The one and only thing that really works in network marketing is the single, bold stroke. It could be a pastor has signed up his complete congregation; a printer has just run 250,000 leaflets through his private circulation magazine, a best-selling author has signed up many of his readers, a guru has put the proposition to his devotees and they ran with it, a car enthusiast has launched it into his AutoClub, a rock bank player has shared it to his audience, an internet marketer writes an informative e-book and sends it to his list of tens of thousands and they love the idea of a biz-opp, a CEO has runs it through his organization, a sales manager has run it through his team, a footballer has shown it to his club, a volunteer has shared it with his charity, a scout master has his troop fly-post every single car in the neighborhood announcing a local biz-opp. Now is the time to get real, grow up, have a wake-up call, a paradigm shift, whatever, because this is exactly what leaders do, and you're looking for leaders – right! Move forward with boldness on your quest to find those leaders and mighty forces will come to your aid and also let the words of the immortal Goethe ring in your ears; Boldness has Genius, Power and MAGIC in it – and in case you forgot, this book is all about Multi Level Magic. Now before you jump to any wild conclusions that sponsoring one-on-one and recruiting individual reps is now redundant, let me remind you what networking is all about: even big networks are built one person at a time, and one who sponsors one, who sponsors one, will ultimately lead to one sponsoring a leader – usually in your depth.

$$$

We have now started to get very serious about building a massive, exciting, *profitable and sustainable* network. Above everything have patience. The immutable laws of network marketing will help you achieve success - and success of course, is the best revenge of all.

PART TWO

SHATTERING THE MYTHS

MYTH: A fiction or half-truth, especially one that forms part of an ideology. A popular belief or story that has become associated with a person, institution, or occurrence. **American Heritage Dictionary**

TRUTH: Reality; actuality. The reality of a situation. A statement proven to be or accepted as true. Conformity to fact or actuality. **American Heritage Dictionary**

WHY SHATTER THE MYTHS?
I think that's a fair question and I'll give you an honest answer from my perspective. I sincerely believe that there is so much guff and hyperbole both inside and outside our industry, I think we need to shatter the myths for once and for all, and uncover what is really going on. Every time we examine a myth and try to get under its skin, we very quickly discover the corollary, like two rabbits ears appearing out of a top hat as if by magic, and that alone

will lead us to gaining clarity of thought, that we as individuals and the industry as a whole, haven't had for a long time. By uncovering the truths, we suddenly have effective rules that we can live by, meaningful things to get duplicated and as a result we become more efficient, and make much more money with far less effort and much more certainty. Hopefully, by the time you finish this module, you will breathe freer and feel that a huge black cloud has been lifted from your shoulders.

MLM MYTH #1 The product has to be consumable

TRUTH: This is an old fashioned viewpoint, probably perpetuated by those selling soap power and other consumables, and for long period of time it did seem to be the case. The truth is, it appears that these days practically anything goes, and for most part very successfully too, including; telecoms, nutrition, water filters, diet, insurance, silver and gold coins, utilities and I have to say, more and more digital products too. I will add here, that the real power of network marketing kicks in when you start pushing the biz-opp rather than the product, because people's real interest is in making money, not spending it.

MLM MYTH #2 Never work outside your pay-line

TRUTH: It seems to me that we have immediately jumped into the deep end here and maybe that's not a bad thing. With a title like Wide 'N Deep we had to address the subject sometime, so we may as well get stuck in now, and what follows is backed up by immutable Law #19: A large *sustainable* income will dictate that a large part of your network will be outside of your immediate pay-line. It amazes me, that when you ask many networkers, even seasoned pros, what 'width' is in their network, they immediately answer by saying, "Width is the people on your front line." Whilst this is absolutely true, the real power of width kicks in on your bottom line, wherever that may be, and that's where the big bucks are made in MLM, so it is worth learning this fundamental truth, right up front. Let me give you a very simple example, by way of illustration only. For our example, let's use a simple network that is three wide, pays eight levels deep and pays a residual $6 a month for everyone in the network. Anyone with any sense at all, will see that the front line will pay out $18 a month, the second line will pay out $72 a month, but the eighth level will pay out circa $36,000 a month, assuming you have filled a complete matrix symmetrically, and you also will pick up

$6 per head on all lines above the eighth level as well. Without working it out in detail, you can very easily see we are talking big money – very BIG money! What I want you to focus on is your bottom line, where ostensibly your MLM jackpot is, your big payday in network marketing is coming from. This is what you aspire to, and that's great. Make BIG money in network marketing, that what it's all about – for sure. But here's the rub, if you have a row of six thousand people on that bottom line, paying you the big money that you richly deserve, how long do you think they will stay there for, if they are not locked in and building and growing a network of their own? Not very long for sure, because Law #16 states that if folk are not locked IN, they will drop OUT. Of course looking at it at first blush, it would seem obvious that you need to keep people up close to you and not let your network grow outside your pay-line, but we should examine it in closer detail, because you are looking to attain an awesome residual income and leave a life-changing legacy for your family, you will want to build your business on a rock solid foundation, one that is one *underpinned* by *massive depth* – albeit outside your immediate pay-line. From this simple little illustration a lot of magic dust appears so let's see if we can get some of it to rub off on to you, because there are salutary lessons here, that are worth learning and acting upon. Later in this module, we'll be discussing these important concepts in depth – get it, in depth!

MLM MYTH #3 You need leaders on your front line

TRUTH: You need three leaders on your front line, or you need six leaders on your front line, is an absolute myth. Let's get to the bottom of this right now because this myth might be one of the big things holding you back like a ten ton anchor, in making your network build and grow, and stopping your full money earning potential. Unfortunately a lot of people believe and say, "I am looking three leaders for my front line, and I am not going to sign up anyone other than leaders, because I know this is the key to making this thing happen." In a way I can understand their logic, because it *almost* makes sense. But alas, it is only theory and a nasty myth that really does deserve to be shattered, because this one alone can hold you back in MLM forever – and forever is a very long time. Now here's the thing: getting leaders on your front line is *not duplicatable* and is also very unlikely to happen – in the real world of MLM. Let's assume for a moment that you were fortunate enough to get three leaders on your front line. Would those three leaders be able to get three leaders each, on their front lines, making a total of nine leaders. Would those nine leaders be able to get three leaders each on their front line, making a total of twenty leaders on that level and a total of forty leaders in the group? I don't think so - no way Jose! Let's take this scenario to its logical conclusion, that of perfect duplication, which means you are going to sign up a complete network full of leaders, in total violation of immutable Law #1: Twenty percent of the people will do eighty percent of the work and sales. It's the way of the world, that there will always more followers than leaders and your network, like all networks, is going to have twenty percent of people who do all the work and the remaining eighty percent will be followers. It is even worth drawing out a complete network of circles, so that you can assimilate this once and for all. Draw one circle at the top of the network which is you, then draw three circles below that, and nine below that, and twenty seven below that, and so on, in the shape of a triangle. Then start filling in the circles with the names of people who are leaders in your eyes; Donald Trump, Robert Kiyosaki, Barak Obama, Richard Branson, Winston Churchill, Bill Gates, Steve Jobs and so forth. Hopefully you will see that filling a complete network full of leaders is not practical, and therefore not duplicatable, therefore why would anyone propagate the myth of getting three leaders on your front line. It's impossible! However, what has emerged from the combined wisdom of top diamonds, and hundreds of millions of hours of networking experience in the field, over a period of six decades, is absolutely profound and it's this: *leaders will come from the depth*. The most expedient way to utilize your resource of people, is to start signing-up as many reps as possible and then watch out for leaders to appear in the depth. This is what actually happens in networking and *this is duplicatable*. How to recognize leaders? Now that's exactly the kind of question that you should be asking! You will find them in the depth when you are going through your monthly print-out or your back office, and there you will see that someone has sponsored three, five, ten, fifty, or however many it is. Potential leaders are those who rock up at every meeting and training, they focus on business and ask questions. You'll hear their names over and over again, these are the leaders in your network, and these are the people you want to be working with, and motivating to do even more, because I can guarantee, out of the people that they sign up, some more leaders will appear in the depth and this is how it happens, over and over again. It's what works in the real world of

MLM and for big success you need to be focusing on what really works, and *exactly what can be duplicated in the real world*, and steering away from debilitating guff, hyperbole and myths – that will keep you *away* from the BIG money in MLM.

As a connoisseur of human nature, I still find it very difficult to judge who will turn out to be a leader in this industry, and decide who will run with it or not. You might think that the sharp professional in a suit with a flashy car parked outside is going to do it because he already has a big business network and that he will run with it, but I can almost promise you that it will be the hippy who rocks up on a moped and starts flying with the thing, or the rich dude who doesn't even he need it, and he will turn out to be your next diamond. It could even be the local bank manager or the guy that doesn't even have a suit that is going to shock you with their explosive growth antics. You can use all the qualification tactics in the world, and I do admit that we try to qualify people, but it's been proven by hundreds of millions of hours by networking in the field, what really happens is that the strangest, most mysterious and unexpected people will do it and the people who you qualify and think will be high flyers won't. Take this on board, because what I am giving you an absolute gem, and if you lock onto this one gem, you can then get on with building your business immediately, and it also means that you can teach and train other people around you to start building their businesses, and not be sitting around waiting for leaders to arrive on your front line, something that hasn't happened in 20, 30, 60 decades in network marketing – and it's certainly not going to start happening now. The leaders come from the depth, and because the cream always rises to the top, the leaders will make themselves known to you, simple as that. Momentum is a major key to gaining traction in this business and this myth has the capability of taking away the initiative to get started. In this tough economic climate, all sorts of people are unemployed and hungry to increase their disposable income and bank managers, brokers, property developers, dentists, ambulance drivers and all manner of people are now getting into network marketing. Don't qualify them too quickly, because even if they are not leaders, one will lead to one, that will lead to one, then suddenly another leader will appear – invariably in your depth. And that's not magic, that's just the way it is.

MLM MYTH #4 It'll never start

TRUTH: Before I shatter this demoralizing myth, I want to tell you a little story that is to do with getting that first person signed up into your network. I do appreciate that after being involved in this industry for over thirty years, that sometimes it is very difficult to get that first person signed into your network and start gaining that initial momentum and traction can be so frustrating and demoralizing. I really do know that – believe me. Getting that first person signed-up is absolutely crucial and I am reminded of the story of the lovely old American couple that came over to the UK to discover their roots. Of all places they ended up in Norfolk, and they tracked down an old village church and enthusiastically started to study grave stones to see if they could find various ancestors names in order to track back in the church's register, to grasp a glimpse of their ancestry. As they were walking around the graveyard, the husband heard this strange hissing noise, so he told his wife, and they went to investigate. As they pushed away some branches, they came across an old train station complete with railway tracks and old steam train that was being worked upon. Coming from America, they were used to the bigger Amtrak electro-diesel trains, and they had never seen a really old fashioned steam train before, and they were in awe. There was a wisp of smoke coming out the chimney stack, a few drops of oil dripping onto the tracks, combined with steam hissing loudly from one of the pipes, and to tell the truth the old hulk didn't look too impressive. The wife looked at her husband and said quizzically; "Waddya you think honey?" and with a dismissive wave of his hand he replied cynically, "It'll never start – it'll never start!" But they didn't know anything about steam trains, or the guy on board who was the fireman who was stoking the boiler as quickly as he could, simultaneously dialing all the brass knobs and tapping dials. He had a red kerchief on his head with a knot in each corner and the sweat was streaming down his coal-blackened face and he still kept shoveling coal into the tender and dialing up all the dials. All of sudden the boiler built up a full head of steam and whistle blew. Outside there was a massive flywheel spinning round, pistons and con-rods belting back and forth, wheels going around as this mechanical marvel burst into life. Frightened out of her skin, the old lady jumped back and shouted loudly, "Waddya do you think *now* honey! Gesticulating wildly her husband screamed back, "It'll never stop - IT'LL NEVER STOP!" I love that story, and I believe networking is just like that. When you first get involved and try to get started, just trying to find that one person to sign as your first rep, you think 'It'll never start…' but believe me, when you have created a critical mass and got a few leaders in your depth, it will never stop, even if you do, and that's the sheer magic of it, and that's what you have got to look forward to. Once you sign one or two onto your front line and they sign one or two onto their front lines who then suddenly find a few leaders in the depth and then your network will never stop building and growing exponentially and that's not just fantastic, it's awesome. Not only that, it'll never stop. Say it with me; "IT'LL NEVER STOP!

MLM MYTH #5 That's not duplicatable
TRUTH: "Don't do that, it's not duplicatable" How many times have I heard that hog wash, invariably followed up by, "You need leaders on your front line." Let's set the record straight for once and for all, and get you back on track of how you are going to build a huge network; get some momentum into your own flywheel, sign-up lots of reps and make some BIG money in network marketing. For sure, this is business where you want to and need to get duplicated, no question about that about. But it is imperative that you get the right things duplicated and immutable Law #14 states that: It is

imperative to teach and train that correct and meaningful things are duplicated. It's really very simple: you just need to sign up reps, and then get those reps to sign up other reps, and then find as many leaders in the depth as you possibly can. What could be simpler? Too many times I have heard a rep say, "Oh, I am going to sign somebody up, and he can get us into a church group." Only to have the upline say, "Oh, don't do that, there isn't anybody else in the network who can do that, it is not duplicatable." Another guy says, "I have a guy down the road a few blocks who has a mail order house and he can start sending out tens of thousands of letters every week." Only to be told, "Don't do that, it's not duplicatable." Another rep is just about to sign an internet marketer that can send out 5,000 emails a month or 10,000 blogs or 50,000 podcasts, only to be told, "Don't do that, it's not duplicatable." Or "I have a public speaker who can really talk up the job for our network" only to be told, "Where in your network will they get people like that from, don't do that, it's not duplicatable." Or "I got this book that I am going to place an advert in and send it ….." and before he has finished his sentence he is told, "Don't do that, it's not duplicable." It makes my blood boil, and this comes from the guy who strictly follows the, 'monkey see - monkey do' routine.

However, what really cracks me up, is that no sooner has he finished saying, "Don't do that" he says, "What you really need is three leaders on your front line." Now I am really in hysterics and falling about laughing, because that's exactly what leaders do: over and over again, they do whatever it takes to get the job marketing done. Simples! They send out 10,000 emails, get an advert in their friend's book or write a persuasive e-book of their own, sponsor the pastor of the local church, sign up everyone at the vintage car club, dig out people with huge databases, winkle out leaders of various organizations, use unbelievable creativity, magic and marketing prowess to create their own big bold moves – and that is exactly what is required to make big money in MLM, and as Law #22 categorically states: The one and only thing that really works in network marketing is the single, bold stroke. Remember what boldness has in it? Genius, power and MAGIC – right! So, just to close the loop on this session until we come back to it from umpteen other angles; what you really want is leaders, mostly of which will come from the depth and when you get them, encourage them to help your network explode, using all sorts of ultra-creative marketing techniques. Does this mean sponsoring one-on-one, one person at a time is redundant? Certainly not! It is the very cement that holds the whole thing together, but what you want duplicated is to get leaders in the depth, who will get out there and market – in as colossal and explosive way as humanly possible! That's how it's done – and that's no myth, it's the truth.

MLM MYTH # 6 MLM won't work in my home town

TRUTH: 'It won't work in my home town' is a complete myth and I can only assume this particular one is perpetuated by networkers who try to make it happen but don't or can't, and then try to justify the reason as to why they failed. I know, it's just an excuse but one that I have heard dozens, if not hundreds of times. "It won't work in my hometown because everybody is retired and no one is looking for business opportunity." Or "It won't work in my hometown because everybody is rich or it won't work because everybody is already employed." But it doesn't really matter why it won't work in any home town because it's just a very lame excuse and I can guarantee there are people looking for a business opportunity and a way to earn extra money or even make a fortune in every town city, town and country - in the world. But of course the real solution is to take the MLM out of your home town as quickly as possible and then it really will be working in your home town, because you will be running your own successful MLM from there. Both Stephen Harris and I operate from small towns in the UK and we chose to take our MLM out of our towns and hit the States, and that is exactly where we spend the majority of our Skype time – and we love it. Modern day communications are brilliant; you have Skype, phone, email, the internet and so much more. What more do you need to get your MLM out of your town, and working in your town, from your town? There is simply no excuse – just a myth that's passed its sell-by-date.

MLM MYTH # 7 You need to sign people on your first meeting

TRUTH: You need to sign prospects on your first meeting, is absolutely wrong, unnecessary and could prove detrimental to the growth of your MLM. The main thing as far as I am concerned, is to build rapport, and to do that I enter the persons inner world and become just like them. There is a chapter on rapport building in my best seller *Talk & Grow Rich*, so grab a copy ASAP, from Kindle, Amazon or Audible. It has been proven beyond doubt that establishing rapport first, before you try to sell, is of paramount importance, but I still see many networkers rushing in and trying it on, before they have built a sound rapport with their prospect. Once I have built a rapport, I then start to feed in the information they need to make an informed decision about the business opportunity. Get your mind around your particular MLM and line up all the marketing collateral, literature and products in advance of the meeting. This is important because all of this material is your silent salesman, and I know that if folk have something to take away this will all help the education process, even when you not there to explain things. The last thing I am worried about is signing people up on the first meeting. I already know from experience that it sometimes takes more than three meetings to sign a new rep, sometimes it's only two, but I do whatever it takes to ensure that the prospect has the information he needs to really understand the opportunity that is in front of him. At the second meeting I will encourage him to bring along his wife or partner along, because on many occasions this can assist the decision making process and move things on apace.

MLM MYTH #8 Isn't that pyramid selling

TRUTH: I have to confess, that every time I hear this expression, and I have heard it hundreds of times, it always conjures up the image of an Egyptian relator complete with gallibaya and fez, standing in front of a pyramid that has a large 'For Sale' sign on it and he's trying hard to sell it. However, MLM is a highly regulated industry, but unfortunately over years, it has got tarred with the pyramid selling brush. At the end of this book I have attached an addendum entitled, 'Isn't that pyramid selling' that I was compelled to write a few years back, in order to answer this question for once and for all. You may want to study it, as it carefully sets out the legal definition of pyramid selling and network marketing. It's worth looking at in detail, because this question will come up repeatedly and having a robust answer, can only help you. This is such a handy tome, that it may be worth your while printing it, so that you have it to hand to show any detractors who, unless you explain to them exactly what pyramid selling really is – are only guessing. With a legal network marketing business, and there and many to choose from, you are paid not to recruit, but to sell a useful product or service at a fair price. There are also many benefits for managing and training your own team, but the primary focus is to sell the product and it usually doesn't matter when you come into the business; you have the same opportunity to make money as anyone else in the network.

MLM MYTH #9 Only the people at the top make money

TRUTH: This is an exciting multi-billion dollar industry and like all industries and businesses, those folk who have been in from the beginning and got in at the early stages and have stuck with it through thick and thin, will no doubt be making more money than those people who join years later. It takes time to make money and it often takes a lot of time to make a lot of money. I believe that when you join an MLM, the opportunity is the same for everyone who joins it, and the majority of compensation plans are geared to pay the most money to those who sponsor; sell, teach, train and build a network, and if you work hard and diligently you can even overtake your sponsor and perhaps some of those further upline, providing of course, that you build a bigger network than them.

MLM MYTH #10 You need to work three deep

TRUTH: This is only theory and has no possible scientific or mathematical reason why this would work and anyone saying this is just guessing. Come back to the immutable laws, and you see the only thing that works is to keep going in a leg until you *actually get duplicated,* which could be the first person, second or third rep that you sponsor, or on the other hand it maybe fourth, fifth or sixth. Recall to mind Law #1 that states quite clearly that: twenty percent of the people will do eighty percent of the work and sales, so this alone will give a clear indication of what is required if you are going to be driving the business to fame and fortune for yourself, or leaving your success up to the whimsical actions or inactions of other people. You need to keep driving depth and sponsoring folk and running with it as hard as you possibly can, but only handing the baton over when someone has really got the message to do the same thing – and that is drive depth until you are properly duplicated, which may *possibly be more than three* deep. Of course we are just scratching the surface here, and because this is the heart of the whole shebang, which we will come back to it again – and again and again and again from every conceivable angle that I can think of.

MLM MYTH #11 You can't control MLM because you're totally reliant on other people

TRUTH: I have heard this total untruth possibly hundreds of times, especially from people who have tried MLM and quit, because it never worked for them, because they relied, erroneously of course, on other people, who for one reason or another, failed to perform. Working in depth overcomes the problem of control unequivocally, because it allows you to completely take the reins of your business and drive it forward. It does this by allowing you to get below others in your network, completely circumventing if necessary; anyone who is in your way, not working at your pace, not working the plan or not doing what they are supposed to be doing - quite legally, morally and ethically. It's not just absolutely magnificent – it is the real magic of MLM, and such an elegant solution too! And of course that is exactly how it should be and can only be, if MLM is to be successful. With the 80-20 rule in play, there can be no other way and Law # 20 sums it up admirably: Working in depth is the ONE and ONLY tool that ensures MLM is a controllable business. But unfortunately, if you haven't be taught and trained how to work in depth and understand the full implications of it, this will not just stunt your growth in MLM, it will sooner or later kill it – stone dead. This is such an important subject, it is covered from every conceivable angle later in this book – so hang on to your top hat, because that really is MAGIC!

MLM MYTH #12 It'll saturate
TRUTH: A lot of people get the false impression that you quickly run out of people. MLM has been going six decades now and it hasn't happened yet. I can think of hundreds of companies that have been trying hard to flood the marketplace and gain market share for years and indeed have advertising budgets running into the hundreds of millions of dollars and not one of them has succeeded. Law #15 dictates; you can never saturate the marketplace with a good product, only bad one, and last but not least, I love veteran Tim Sales take on it, in Zig Ziglar's *Network Marketing for Dummies,* and he offers the best argument against the saturation myth. He asks, "Do you know anyone who doesn't have a refrigerator? No? That doesn't stop GE from manufacturing and selling more of them."

MLM MYTH #13 You have to sponsor vast numbers of people to succeed

TRUTH: This industry revolves around a network of people, all doing their own fair share of work, and a small volume of sales. The whole idea is that you don't have to sponsor vast amounts of people to succeed, but everyone sponsors just a few people and then teaches and trains those few people, how to do the same. What makes the whole thing work however, is that when someone becomes proficient at networking and sponsoring, they get into the zone, and they tend to become leaders and operate a two pronged approach of sponsoring and helping those in the depth. I have seen numerous leaders just sponsor literally a handful of reps; and then put all their work, effort and bold creativity into driving depth and building hugely successful networks.

MYTH #14 You have to get in early to be successful

TRUTH: MLM is a serious business and has huge potential no matter whether you joined in the early days of whether you join now. Like all business, MLM takes time to develop and make a lot of money, so the sooner you start the sooner you too will be successful. Because of all the variables involved a fair number of MLM companies close their doors within a few years of opening, so it may make sense not to get in too early, and see which way the wind blows. Maybe the more pragmatic plan is let the company pass the test of time, sort out its teething problems, develop the marketing collateral and then see who is earning what, and work out an action plan from there.

MYTH #15 I don't have the time or money to get started

TRUTH: If you want to start a business, any business, you need to get your priorities right and that means first and foremost, over and above everything else, making a decision of how to free up precious time and how to acquire sufficient funding to get started. To say you can't do either is just a myth. The heroes who do make a start usually do so by giving up watching television and that action alone will free off huge blocks of time, that heretofore have been frittered away. Next, the heroes go about getting hold of some working capital to give their business a kick-start, and like all businesses, MLM *does* need some kind of wherewithal, especially in the early days, until you gain some traction and it becomes self-sustaining. Best starting point could be a loan from the bank of Ma & Pa or alternatively have a yard sale or car boot sale and get rid of all the stuff in your attic, garage or basement. I remember doing all of the above and more at one time or another including selling my beloved gun collection, cashing in some life policies, remortgaging my house, remortgaging my mother's house - only joking, selling my cherished Aston Martin, all to get working capital to get businesses up and running. Whatever it takes – right!

MLM MYTH #16 No one really gets rich in network marketing

TRUTH: In MLM there are plenty of people making small amounts and large amounts of disposable income every month. The attraction of MLM businesses, it that they allow you to build a residual income and also leave an ongoing legacy for your family. The network marketing industry turns over a hundred billion dollars annually, with a large percentage of that money being paid back to the reps in the field by way of commissions, bonuses, percentages and profit share. If you follow this link, you will see many of the top earners in the industry and the potential that is available to anyone who really goes for it: http://bit.ly/1zSJr9H

MLM MYTH #17 Network marketing is a cult.
TRUTH: The definition of cult: system of religious beliefs. Definition of business: a commercial; activity engaged in as a means of livelihood. I think these are two very distinct statements and it's difficult to see how you could confuse one for the other. However, I have witnessed people who are extremely successful in business, not exclusively MLM, and invariably they are passionate about the product and services they promote. Furthermore, these business leaders are usually dynamic, charismatic, persuasive, sometimes to the point of being evangelical, and are good communicators and love to help other people make money and become successful. I don't know whether it's too much estrogen in the water, booze or drugs or perhaps a cocktail, but I must confess that these days, I find far too many people, talking far too much gibberish for my liking. So much so, you have to be careful, because if you're not, you end up thinking that it's the norm and what they are saying is probably true. In MLM, above everything else, do your own thinking.

MLM MYTH #18 You're not selling, you're just sharing

TRUTH: The American Heritage Dictionary describes Marketing, thus: To deal in a market; engage in buying or selling. To try to make a product or service appealing to particular groups of consumers; promote by marketing. The American Heritage Dictionary describes Business as: The activity of buying and selling commodities, products or services. In MLM you definitely need to sell the products because immutable Law #8 dictates that if the products don't sell, no one earns a bean. Further, MLM is a business opportunity and that's a fact that you cannot, and should not get away from, because that's exactly what people are looking for; an opportunity to sell products and services, whereby they can make some money for themselves. I think this myth is potentially very dangerous, because we are trying to sell more and more product and yet we are steering newbies further and further way from the truth: no work involved, no selling required - only sharing; but the moment they come on board, they see with their own eyes, what is required of them. Why perpetuate a myth, when steering people into learning the skills and strategies that they will need, would serve them better?

MLM MYTH #19 MLM is not serious business
TRUTH: MLM is both a serious and very exciting business that shifts over $80-$100-billion worth of products and services a year, depending whose figures you believe, and it engages millions of people and operates in the US; UK, Australia, Japan, all over Europe and just about every other country in the world. Network marketing and referral marketing is used by major corporates like Time-Warner, Gillette, Colgate-Palmolive, Lillian Vernon, Citigroup and MLM is endorsed by the likes of Donald Trump, Robert Kiyosaki and Zig Ziglar and at least half a dozen MLMs are publicly listed companies. To me this denotes very serious business, and if it isn't, I don't know what is.

MLM MYTH #20 You have to sell door-to-door and host parties
TRUTH: There are a goodly number of MLMs where selling door-to-door and parties feature quite high on the list of things to do, but there are also many opportunities that have nothing to do with the foregoing. A little research will lead you into an MLM where you have an affinity with the product and a marketing method that suits your

own particular personality. If there's anything we've learned from the history of network marketing it is this: the average amount of product individual networkers sell on a monthly basis is minimal, and that leaves plenty of room for improvement. One thing is for sure, the product has to sell and it would be great if we could just double the small volume of sales that everyone makes in a network, then the reps would earn twice the amount, on the same number of people. Get ultra-creative in your sales endeavors and try party plan, door-knocking, product demos and whatever bold tactics you can think of.

MLM MYTH #21 MLM is one of those 'get rich quick schemes' that doesn't work

TRUTH: It is unfortunate that there are so many get rich quick schemes, ponzi's, chain-letters, money-go-rounds and internet scams that tend to do the rounds and undoubtedly attract more than their fair share of victims. These schemes are often fueled by greed and naiveté, tend to grow rapidly for a few months, maybe even a few years before they fizzle out, leaving a trail of financial debris in their wake that usually takes the victims a long to time to recover from, and frequently leaves a bad taste in their mouths about network marketing. Genuine MLMs are totally different insofar as a product or service is being sold and reordered on a regular basis and they usually operate with total transparency, which I think that is not only admirable, but also common sense. With even the smallest amount of due-diligence, delving into what could be a scam, you usually can spot umpteen flaws that will set alarm bells ringing, and it's these flaws that sooner or later will prove to be the scams demise.

MLM MYTH #22 You can do this in one hour a week
TRUTH: MLM is both serious and very exciting business and true of all businesses, what you get out of it, will depend very much upon what you put in. The business revolves around meetings and you should attend all of the biz-opp meetings and training meetings in your area and more importantly take people to those meetings so they can be exposed to the business. Further, you should be continually list building and consistently and persistently pitching your own warm market. Once you have a few reps signed in your depth, you would then be working the warm market of those people too. There is plenty to go at in the business and if you want to make BIG money in MLM I

suggest that you make yourself *very* busy – doing the right things of course. All out massive action, for all out massive profit, – and it's highly doubtful that you could do too much massive action in one hour a week - I know that I can't!

MLM MYTH #23 No one wants to help you once you have signed up

TRUTH: This is myth and utter nonsense because in theory every single person in the upline, leading right back to the company, should want to help the new rep in multiple ways. Now if this isn't happening, there is something dramatically wrong, because this is what networking is all about and how it works; and in essence it is the number one deed that we get paid for: helping, teaching and training others. This book is dedicated to teaching and training those things that are not just missing; but most folk in MLM are absolutely oblivious to, namely: new reps need to be made aware that they need to seek help upline, if they are not receiving it from their immediate sponsor, who may very well be new to the business, and not fully trained and competent to do so. The second point: in many instances there is practically no awareness in uplines, that they must keep working with and driving depth and teaching and training in depth, and not just assuming someone else is doing it. There needs to be far more education about reps being too precious about *'their people'* because in the long term this is a formula for disaster, and is covered in detail later in the module. New reps need to be given the comfort that although the upline will help them 'seal the deal', the new person will be signed up under the introducing rep, and not hijacked or stolen.

MLM MYTH # 24 Within ten years, 95% of all products sold will be via MLM
TRUTH: Although direct sales and MLM account for $100 billion in global sales annually, it would be a long way to go before sales are into the trillions of dollars, which of course would be the figure if 95% of sales of all products were conducted through MLM. Maybe the people who propagate this myth are really saying that all *types* of products will be sold via MLM, which is something totally different of course, but very conceivable.

MLM MYTH #25: Harvard and Wharton teach courses on MLM

TRUTH: The truth is that Harvard and Wharton have never taught courses on MLM but my research indicates that in the USA there is a community college in Kansas, called Bethany College that does. This myth was probably perpetuated by someone trying to add some credibility to the industry, but unwittingly detracted from it.

MLM MYTH #26 Slow and steady wins the race

TRUTH: This is first and foremost a people business and speed and momentum are crucial to building and maintaining a network. As long as things are *happening* and there is growth, people tend to stick around. However, they will not stay with you indefinitely if there is no activity in their depth. Some networks have the ability to allow you to keep new sign-ups on your front line, for perhaps a sixty-day holding period, before you place them strategically in your network. The thinking behind this, is to see whether they are going be one of your leaders or not, so you can keep them up close and personal to you, or decide to place them in the depth. In essence that person is just sitting; assuming of course he is not sponsoring and selling in his own right, he is therefore doing no work at all. On the other hand, is he were placed in the depth of your network, immediately he would be doing *extremely valuable* work, locking in one or more of the team and motivating them too, just by his presence. It's all a delicate balancing act, but my personal preference is to be thinking strategically all the time about making every team member count and extracting the maximum amount of work potential from passives. If they turn out to be super stars, or leaders that begin tearing up trees, that is great too – no matter where they are in your network.

MLM MYTH #27 Impossible to earn big money in MLM as the chain will break

TRUTH: Most MLM compensation plans are very well conceived so that if people quit, there is usually full compression so that everyone moves up a notch. In this way, the chain or link can never be broken, and most modern MLM software assures that it can't be.

MLM MYTH #28 Many home-based network businesses offer false promises

TRUTH: This statement is trite but true: If something sounds too good to be true, then it probably is. I see many business opportunities not just MLMs, that are over eagerly promoted with false and wild claims. Add this to the propensity for people tending to hear what they want to hear and interpret things that are said to suit their own version and meaning of the world. When exploring a business opportunity, it is always best to hear the presentation from three different individuals within the organization and ask many people about the opportunity before making a commitment. MLM is an exciting and lucrative business and warrants a well thought through plan of action of how you are going to commit to the business and make it a success for yourself. Make the decision to become a player within the industry and harness all of your own personal power and skills and then focus to make it a successful venture. If you make *that* decision, the Wide 'N Deep series will be there to assist you every step of the way in realizing your full ambition, every dream and every aspiration.

MLM MYTH #29 It takes a certain type to succeed in MLM

TRUTH: Over the years I have seen all types of people from all walks of life, ethnic background, every race and creed become successful within our industry - *providing* they stick to the laws and principles that govern success. They used to say that if a prospect could fog up a mirror, that would be a good starting point as any, but I tend to do some qualification, before I rush in and sign someone in my network. I try to ascertain whether they will be a good follower so they can learn the business. I make sure that they have the wherewithal to pay the monthly commitment fee and ongoing costs until they gain some traction, and I want to make sure they have sufficient time for biz-opp meetings, trainings and three way Skype calls. In other words, I am not necessarily looking for someone to fog up a mirror, but preferably someone who has got a little oil in their lamp.

MLM MYTH #30 You'll lose all your friends and destroy relationships

TRUTH: Personally speaking, I have made far more many friends than those that I have lost. Now I come to think of it, I don't think I have lost any friends at all, but certainly gained many. I think the people who do lose friends, and I am sure there are some, is probably due to their insensitive approach, bad timing and not learning the necessary skillsets before trying to make things happen. I picked up the idea and have the goal of 'having a million friends' from fellow MLM author and speaker John Kalench, shortly before his untimely death. I shared the stage with John many times and I recommend all of his books, but start with, *Being the Best you Can be in MLM*.

MLM MYTH #31 MLMs have inferior and expensive products

TRUTH: Over the years we have seen a number on MLMs go into the billions of dollars quite quickly and many others have the potential to do so. The reason why they have done this is that they have exceptional, value for money, high quality products that there is a demand for. Of course there is always an exception to the rule and those pushing inferior and expensive products tend not to pass the test of time.

MLM MYTH #32 You have to be a super-salesman to make it work

TRUTH: I don't believe you have to be super-salesman to succeed in MLM, but what I do believe however, is that you will need to develop some specific skillsets if you haven't already got them. These are skills that any reasonable person, over a period of time, with study and diligence can acquire. Skills like; making a logical but enthusiastic presentation and closing skills that will give you the ability to seal-the-deal. Motivational skills that will give you the ability to empower others and help them discover their full potential and own leadership skills. Becoming disciplined and punctual and getting yourself to meetings – all of them, with other folk in tow. These are the skills are required, without a doubt, but they are MLM skillsets, not necessarily super-salesman skills.

MLM MYTH #33 You have to know a lot of people to succeed in MLM

TRUTH: I always find this amusing because it's impossible to reach the age of twenty, thirty, forty, fifty, sixty without knowing a lot of people, and even if you were brought up in cave you'd still know people. I think what people are saying here is that, "I am too embarrassed to pitch my family and friends, of which I have dozens, on the opportunity, because I burned them last time around and that biz-opp never went anywhere." The truth is, that every rep has to overcome their shyness, embarrassment, laziness and get stuck into the *essence* of the business which is *talking* to people, particularly your warm market, the warm market of your network and all other folk - without exception or exclusion. That's why they call it word-of-mouth marketing and even if you don't have a warm market of your own, you still have over six billion other folk to go at – and if you can't do that, it's probably time to go back to picking strawberries.

MLM MYTH #34 Building an MLM business using the internet is impossible

TRUTH: A few of the old school are still mighty resistant to the internet and say this is because MLM is primarily a relationship business, and it cannot be conducted online using modern technologies. I am old school myself, having been involved in MLM for over thirty five years, and I have also been heavily involved with the internet since day one. I am pretty sure that when the automobile was introduced, there were those who still favoured the horse and buggy and probably hung onto the reins and shovel as long as they could. Likewise, there was probably resistance by some to the airplane; radio, television, fax machine, cell phone and even the computer. But I am sure that we all agree, they have found their way into everyday life. There is great video by Eric Worre, author of GO

PRO, which by the way, is a must read for serious networkers, and he talks about people abusing the system by using email willy-nilly and spamming everyone, and I agree with him wholeheartedly that this outrageous behaviour has to stop – what's more it is totally unnecessary. The more the internet develops, the more efficient it is becoming and it responds to niches and highly targeted and sophisticated marketing, *not* the shotgun approach. Harnessing the internet is of vital importance to our industry and remember: Law #11: Harness modern technologies and communications or slip behind, which, by the way is immutable. Sure that lots of the old school have been opposed to doing traditional network marketing online for a long time now, however, the trade winds are changing rapidly and more and more is being done on-line and I suspect the younger set are doing more so, maybe even exclusively. Stephen Harris and I are based predominantly in the UK, but are building a huge network in the US and most of this is done by lead generation on the internet, followed up by email and Skype calls. The internet is so important, that Wide 'N Deep books #4, #5 and #6 in this series will be dedicated to showing you how to really harness its awe-inspiring power and everything allied to it, so much so, you really will be able to sit in front of your screen and Click & Grow Rich, which by the way, is the subtitle of Wide 'N Deep #4 which is coming your way at the speed of light, in Kindle, Paperback and Audio format.

MLM MYTH #35 You can just set up your business and forget about it

TRUTH: This is a business whereby you need to get some serious momentum into the flywheel and believe me that takes hard work, effort, mental energy, focus and diligence. You need to get that critical mass together of 10-20 people, signed-up, *motivated* and raring to go. They need to be taught and trained in the power-of-one so they too can get their first rep on board. Once you have momentum in the flywheel, you'd be well advised to keep your foot on the accelerator and keep sponsoring one-on-ones yourself and working very hard in the depth, teaching, training, motivating and unlocking your reps problems, no matter how trivial they may seem to you, and building momentum even more. All this time you'll be consolidating your network, building depth and creating security – the day will come when you will be able to forget about your network, but by this time, you will not want to!

MLM MYTH #36 You get rich in MLM by spending no money at all

TRUTH: Like all businesses, you have to prime the pumps to gain traction. This is a marketing business and marketing costs money. Although this is primarily a 'word-of-mouth' business, you still need marketing collateral; brochures, products, samples, tools and enough money to pay for travel to training meetings and events. A further investment on personal development is highly recommended and a weekly supplement of positive thinking books, audios and DVDs, many of which can be seen on YouTube, can immunize the system and get you over the humps and hurdles and through hoops of fire that you will face, as you drive your business forward. After forty year five years, I am still investing *heavily* in my own education and have no intention of stopping – ever!

MLM MYTH #37 MLM is so simple anyone can do it

TRUTH: MLM is a life changing industry and you start a proper business from day one, without too much capital outlay. Like all home businesses, you have to start from scratch and build and grow it. This is people a business and developing people skills is paramount, and the more of these that you have, the more you will excel in the business. This is also teamwork business and unfortunately many entrepreneurs want to do it all themselves, but MLM doesn't work like that. You don't want to be the manager that does everything himself. Get into the spirit of learning the skills first, and then teaching and training those skills to others. By acting as a team, you can leverage off each other skillsets. Like a football team, many times players work out their own particular strengths and play to them. In our group we have a presenter who does great job, he loves speaking in public and wows the audience every time and there are always people in the wings picking up his skills. Then we have a greeter who shakes people's hands when they arrive at a biz-opp meeting and others who love organizing Skype calls and webinars and others put on ham and beans days. So even if you don't have these skillsets to begin with, by turning up to all the biz-opp and training meetings and bringing people with you, *and being part of a team,* you will learn by osmosis, and over period of time, you too will learn the ropes.

MLM MYTH #38 There's no work or selling involved
TRUTH: This myth is perpetuated by reps trying to get folk into their networks at any cost, and sometimes by deception. Of course there's work to be done, the same as any other legitimate business and the harder you work, the luckier you get. I know many of the real heavyweights in the industry and they embrace it as a lifestyle business and it all ends up being one massive merry-go-round of fun; travel, events, meeting new ambitious people and motivating them to reach their full potential, helping reps attain their goals, exploring new countries and locations, dinners out, having even more fun – and is always on hand to help a new rep sign up his first distributor.

MLM MYTH # 39 MLM is for people who can't get a real job
TRUTH: I do believe that many moons ago MLM was frowned upon by many entrepreneurs saying that it was just like 'paint by numbers' and it was for people who

couldn't run a real business of their own. These days MLM has so many product options and variations of the theme, and as an industry it has passed the test of time with flying colors. It is viewed by many, including myself, as a very serious opportunity and one that will test all the skills that you already possess and others that you will need to acquire, if you are going to make big money. These days you can see doctors, fireman, clerks, lawyers, carpenters, bankers, lay preachers, pastors, truck drivers, salesmen, florists and just about every vocation you could possibly think of involved in our exciting industry – welcome aboard.

MLM MYTH #40 I'll build your downline for you

TRUTH: This is just a ploy that many people use when recruiting. "There's no work involved, I'll build your network for you, all you have to do is pick up the checks." Many times the ploy backfires because very quickly the new rep discovers there is work to be done, especially if you want to get rich in network marketing. One thing that I think is quite legitimate and also extremely motivating is to say, "I'll drive one of your legs for you, if you drive the other, and I'll match you pace for pace." Driving power legs is relatively simple and all you have to do is keep driving depth in one leg, the power leg. Everyone in that leg gets boost, because you are driving it and what each rep in it has to do is drive another leg, and try to keep up with you. We'll address what happens if they don't or can't, later on in the module.

MLM MYTH #41 The industry has a totally acceptable churn rate

TRUTH: The industry churn rate is totally unacceptable and something needs to be done about it right now. It's hard to put a figure on what it really is, but current research would indicate that it is between 85% and 95% which is a very inefficient way to run a business. It means that in practical terms, folk are leaving by the back door, quicker than you can get them in through the front door. We'll address this serious issue in depth, later in the module and together, acting as a mastermind group, we'll come up with some very pragmatic, ingenious and magical solutions, to get things back on track.

MLM MYTH #42 If you sponsor a leader, the battle is won

TRUTH: You are seeking leaders and it is *highly* likely that the majority of your leaders, if not all of them, will come from the depth of your network. However, having signed a leader who is going to run with it, is just the beginning of the process. Even if the guy is a heavyweight and has a loyal following, remember that he is still a newbie in the business, even if he is recruiting people very quickly. Most upliners are in awe of leaders and their mouths drop open as they watch the new leader sign in bucket loads of new reps. The natural reaction is to say "Wow, he knows what he's doing, let him get on with it." That is usually a big mistake - huge. Invariably what happens, is that all these new reps fail to get taught and trained properly, and just go along with the leader who they have a rapport with. When the leader has finished signing up his loyal band of followers; whether they are from a church congregation, a book fan base or an auto-club is irrelevant, but what usually happens next is this: all those people do not have the group of followers that their leader had, so they each need to find individuals to sign into the business. And they have to keep on doing that until one day they too find a leader, usually in the depth of their business. Of course they probably haven't been diligently taught and trained in the power-of-one, and why should they? The newbie leader probably didn't know that crucial step, of how to train them put all their mental and physical energy into signing up their first rep and what will happen usually is that the network will begin to recede. The antidote of course, is that no matter who the new leader is who has signed all these new reps; the upline leader or leaders should jump down in the depth and start teaching and training how to get find one and sign one, then teach him how to find one and sign one, which of course will ultimately lead to the next leader. Simples!

PART THREE

FORENSICALLY EXAMINING CHURN RATE

WHY PEOPLE QUIT MLM

For thousands of years the vast majority of the global population believed that the World was flat, the Sun travelled around the Earth, and that the Earth was only 6,000 years old, and although we now know for sure that the World is round, the Earth travels around the Sun and the Earth is 4.5 billion years old, I am absolutely convinced that there are many people out there, maybe even some MLMers, who still believe otherwise. There are many sciences that have allowed us to get to the bottom of things and today's modern forensics is one of those that allow us to explore things in minute detail, and not necessarily believe consensus of opinion, until it has been absolutely proven. By using such an approach, this will allow us to bring MLM into the 21st century and give industry leaders something of substance to build upon.

Having been involved in MLM the arena for over thirty years, I am still in awe of the massive churn rate within our industry, in my opinion much of which is unnecessary and can be greatly improved upon. However, through analysis and research, over a long period of time, I believe I that have got to the core of 'churn rate' and discovered the truth, much of which may surprise you. There has been much written on the subject, by both pro and anti-MLMers, much of what I consider to be guesswork, or written by people with hidden agendas, of which there are many. I believe that too much 'skirting around the edges' has been done for far too long and because this is such a serious issue for our industry it cannot be tolerated any longer. Before I launch into the individual reasons why people quit MLM, I think that a look at the much broader picture will help us get our minds around the overall problem. There will always be more followers than leaders and as we have seen from the 80-20 rule you can expect leaders to excel, but the *majority* in any quest, not just MLM, will fail, quit, walk away or generally do their own thing. Many people's lives are completely chaotic, as indeed are their thinking and decision making processes, and getting into an MLM is just as easy as getting out of one. "It felt right at the time – but it isn't right for me now" is a throw-away comment, frequently heard from quitters. On top of that, we have already seen that MLMs attract folk who want to make money; many of which are not suitably equipped to run a business, many with the wrong aptitude; lack of capital, untrainable, not good followers, cannot afford the marketing materials or monthly commitment, too busy with a day job, fire-fighting or other commitments and the list goes on. All of the foregoing creates a recipe for disaster, before we even start to build a network and make money.

Let's take a cursory glance at a few of the superficial reasons why people quit MLM, and then let's get stuck into the core of the problem, with a view to dramatically reducing the unacceptable churn rate, that our industry has become accustomed to, but is no longer acceptable.

SOME SUPERFICIAL REASONS WHY PEOPLE QUIT MLM

Superficial: Of being on the surface, concerned only with what is obvious or apparent. Not thorough or complete. Not deep, serious or profound. Seeming at first glance. **American Webster dictionary**

I QUIT MYTH #1 I got no upline support
Remedy: Many times the new rep doesn't even realise that he can gain help from many different people other than the person who actually sponsored him, and that person, if he is new to MLM himself, may know little or nothing about the business. Creating awareness amongst new reps, that they should seek support further upline is one of many steps that can be and should be taken to ensure all the help, support and correct knowledge is passed to the new rep in a timely manner.

I QUIT MYTH #2 I couldn't sign first rep
Remedy: This is interesting, because no one in MLM should have to sign reps, until they are fully trained and

totally competent in doing do. This rep should have been taught not to try to sign people on his own, but encouraged to get people on three way calls or attend biz-opp meetings with his prospects where there is upline support that is qualified to help the new rep sign in his first rep, or even many of his new reps. This rep has been trying to do something he probably can't do and shouldn't be doing, and he should have his hand held by someone somewhere in the upline, until he is competent enough to close the business himself.

I QUIT MYTH #3 I got a more enticing offer

Remedy: Gold bauble syndrome is everywhere, and certainly no more prevalent than our own industry. Reps talk to colleagues and friends and of course everyone is pitching everyone else on their particular opportunity. Combine that with a streaming avalanche of tantalising offers that come flooding in over the internet every day, that are copy-written by greedy little goblins who live in fairyland, and it's no wonder the industry loses people in droves, on daily basis. New reps should be ingratiated day one, to be alert to 'dream-stealers' and 'gold baubles' and be told over and over again, to stick with one opportunity and get help building the critical mass that is needed in order for growth to happen. This business is a constant educational process and that needs to come from the upline at every opportunity, every single day, because the competition operates relentlessly - 24-7-365.

I QUIT MYTH #4 I couldn't afford the monthly payment

Remedy: It depends if rep in question has lost his job and is only temporarily unemployed and can't afford his payment, or is there a most sinister reason lurking in the background. If the rep is keen stay on board, and build and grow his MLM business, perhaps he can get short term bank loan or more preferably a loan from the bank of Ma & Pa, to tide him over. The more sinister reason could be that his sponsor doesn't properly qualify those that he signs up, and keeps sponsoring downwards, instead of trying to find those who have a steady income or at least some wherewithal. If you keep sponsoring downwards, sooner or later you'll end up in cardboard city – for the unworldly wise, that's where the homeless live in cardboard boxes. Sponsor the greedy – not the needy!

I QUIT MYTH #5 I was promised false hope of easy, quick and early money

Remedy: In an endeavour to sponsor new blood into their business many new reps frequently indulge in 'over-egging the pudding'; telling falsehoods about easy pickings, big earnings and of 'no work to be done'. Of course, sooner or later, all of this will come back to haunt them when the newly sponsored rep realizes that there is work to be done, and a critical mass needs to be built before the big pay checks come flooding in. The remedy is that the educational message about working hard, sticking with it, attend all training meetings and bring two new people to biz-opp meetings. This message has to come at new reps from every angle and like most things in marketing, that message too, has to be heard at least seven times, before it has any impact.

I QUIT MYTH #6 I didn't understand what I had to do

Remedy: Millions of new reps in MLM don't know exactly what to do and that's why many struggle to sign their first rep, and then ultimately leave. When I left school at the tender age of fourteen I signed as an apprentice carpenter and joiner and I finished it on my twentieth birthday. It takes time to learn life skills; and if you want to become a doctor, lawyer or an accountant it may take you even longer. Depending on age, previous experience and skills, a typical newbie will take 12-18 months to acquire MLM product knowledge, pitching and closing skills before he gains any traction at all, let alone start to fly. He needs to be told this early on in his MLM apprenticeship and told it over and over again, and also that many great leaders invariably started out by being good followers.

I QUIT MYTH #7 I got too many rejections

Remedy: Done properly it's difficult to see how this could happen because up until the rep becomes proficient in pitching and closing skills, he shouldn't be getting any rejection at all. He should be introducing new people to three ways calls or biz-opp meetings and letting his skilled and experienced upline do the presentations and all the hard work – and also receiving the rejections, if there are any to be had. If the newbie really has had lots of rejections, a number of people in the upline have not being do their job, the one job incidentally that we earn big money for in MLM – teaching, training, hand-holding and passing on appropriate skillsets to all in the downline, right up until they become proficient to carry out the business in their own right. Leaders needs to amplify the message of teaching and training and ensure the correct message is available in every formant; video, DVDs, audios, brochures, pamphlets, books, e-books and so there is absolutely no excuse of not knowing of how this business should be conducted.

I QUIT MYTH #8 I was not committed, I was easily distracted and not motivated

Remedy: Success in any walk of life, usually takes a clear vision *and* a laser beam focus and determination to follow through, and those attributes usually have to be learned. Those who excel within the MLM industry intuitively inject massive doses of personal development into their programs. Above everything, this is people industry, a teaching and training industry and helping to draw out the potential in people is a major part of the job that we have to do, in order to make the big bucks in MLM. Leaders can steer their teams into a cornucopia of self-help and motivational books; YouTube videos and all manner of inspirational and aspirational materials. There is so much good stuff out there, you can be spoilt for choice, but here's a good starting point: *Skill with People* – Les Giblin, *How to Win Friends and Influence People* – Dale Carnegie, *Millionaire Secrets* and *Talk & Grow Rich* by Ron G Holland, *Think and Grow Rich* – Napoleon Hill.

I QUIT MYTH #9 I spend too much time watching TV
Remedy: The official viewing time is 2.8 hours a day for the average American and that totals nineteen and a half hours a week, which is more than sufficient time to gain some super traction in an MLM of your choice. Individuals have to make a choice here, and I personally gave up TV viewing way back when, and have never looked back. I may watch ten minutes a day, but I soon get bored, simply because there is so much exciting stuff to do; write books, read, ride motorcycles, travel, drive fast cars, collect silver and gold coins, tune motorcycle engines, walk in the hills, star-gaze, swim - or whatever it is that is *your* particular passion. Uplines need to coach, train, persuade and educate downlines that there is an exciting lifestyle to be had, but that will never happen for you as a spectator, only as a participant.

I QUIT MYTH #10 My friend or sponsor has dropped out

Remedy: When this happens, the upline that has their wits about them will jump in and befriend the person so they have a shoulder to cry on and someone new that they can rely on and trust. The upline that *really* has their wits about them will have *already* befriended that person by working in depth with them and that person would realize that they have many more friends in the network than the person who actually sponsored them. There is usually nowhere near enough working in depth, which incidentally, is ONLY thing that makes MLM a controllable business and that is what this book is primarily about.

I QUIT MYTH #11 There are no meetings in my local area

Remedy: When the rep joined the business, their sponsor and upline should have made clear all the many options available. Communication in this business is crucial and if doesn't always have to come from your own personal sponsor. Many times there will be no physical meetings in specific areas, but that mustn't stop you travelling to meetings, or the flow of virtual meetings. We have people in our group who regularly travel up to sixty miles to get to particular meetings, and in the States I envisage that they travel even further. Stephen Harris and I sponsor people all over the States from our respective bases in the UK and continually hook up with our people on Skype, phone and email.

I QUIT MYTH #12 I didn't have a big enough dream
Remedy: Teaching people how to think big and how to dream is a pivotal part of what we do. It's what we get paid for. Finding out individual reps dreams and aspirations and turning them ON to be goal oriented is an exciting part of the challenge and journey. Once they realize that MLM is a vehicle for accomplishing really big dreams, they then have to be taught how to break goals in down into smaller chunks, that can be *visualized* then *actualized*. People will not reach their full potential until they learn to break down larger goals and start accomplishing smaller goals first, that all lead them in the right direction of the big dreams. Breaking down awe-inspiring goals that require the income from a massive network, can easily be assimilated by knowing that even the largest networks are built one person at a time.

I QUIT MYTH #13 I didn't have a WHY

Remedy: Everyone has a different reason for wanting to build a substantial business and make a lot of money, and I think it is extremely motivating to turn people ON to their own particular and personal WHY. You can ask, "WHY am I doing this?": to get my kid through college, so I can be financially independent, so my parents don't have to work anymore, so I can travel the world, so I can explore the States in an RV, so I can work when I want - where I want - with who I want, to leave a legacy for my children, so I can take a nine month sabbatical in Australia, so that I can build my eight bedroom dream house complete with pool, so I can buy a houseboat in Africa, so I can leave lots of money to my favourite charity, so that I can – and this is the important one; do whatever it is that I want to do, and own what I want to own. Once you have discovered your own personal WHY, it is the much easier to create a fool-proof plan and roadmap for getting there and cultivating the stick-ability to ensure that you actually arrive.

I QUIT MYTH #14 I wasn't welcomed as a team member

Remedy: Uplines should be looking out for new faces who roll up to meetings and engage in conversation with them, and not rely solely on the person that introduced them to the meeting in the first place. If you are a newbie it is the first job of your sponsor to warmly introduce you to the members of the upline as a very important person and currently, in most networks, there is simply not enough of this happening. It is quite understandable that a prospect or newbie rep may not know that huge upline support is available – or *should* be available. On the other hand, there is absolutely no excuse whatsoever, for anyone who has been in the MLM business, to know that its sole function is to operate as a team, and teach and train the newbies until they are competent to sponsor in their own right. The new prospect, or newbie rep needs to feel warmly welcomed as part of that team from day one, and needs to know that he can go *anywhere* upline for help, advice mentoring, hand-holding, motivation and training. Ostensibly, every single person leading right back to the company in the upline, is directly or indirectly earning on that person, no matter how far downline they are.

I QUIT MYTH #15 Somebody stole my dream

Remedy: There is an over-abundance of negativity in the world and if you can alert team members that there will always be detractors out there trying to put you down, steal your dream and tell you that you are doing the wrong thing - they will at least be prepared for it and know how to handle it. I find that most folk are extremely resilient, and what usually happens is that when someone quits an MLM because someone stole their dream, it won't be too long before they go find another mountain to climb, and start over. Knowing this is very useful, because if you spot the signs of someone who is thinking of quitting, you can get in there first, and deliver a pep-talk about stickability, being part of the winning team that they already know, and making things happen together. Pep-talks, encouragement, praise, fostering care, attention to individuals, team work, TLC are things to be dished out by the bucket-load, on a day-to-day basis – and the sole reward for doing so, is that you become a BIG money earner in MLM.

I QUIT #16 I became totally disillusioned because wasn't told a proper story

Remedy: Uplines should always be extremely articulate at open meetings and on Skype calls and Webinars as to what the real deal is, and what the real story is, early on in the days of a new rep coming on board. Uplines must assume that the newbie has not heard the full and true story of what the business is all about, so he must immediately start, in a very user friendly manner, to manage expectations and explain in detail that this is a proper business that offers substantial rewards and there is a job of work to be done. The upline can then get into list building and working a warm market and how the newbie rep can get his people to biz-opp meetings or Skype calls or three way calls to help him close his business until he confident to do so on his own. In my experience, newbie reps give an almighty sigh of relieve when they get past all the hyperbole and noise and discover *exactly* how the business operates and *exactly* what they have to do in order to make an MLM take off, and that there are specific procedures in place and jobs of work to be done.

I QUIT MYTH #17 I lack motivation

Remedy: If ever there was a situation where motivation plays an overwhelming role, it is within the MLM arena. Not everyone is a self-starter and automatically motivated to get on with things and not everyone knows *exactly* what to do next – without being shown. For most people it is much more complicated than that, and getting motivated is usually a learned response. For the longest time now I have realized that most people need and also like constant reminders: have you set some large and small goals, do you read them aloud and visualize them every day, have you got a dream scrap book, have you got a picture your of dream car, dream house and other big goals on your refrigerator door, have you got a vision board with a collage of all your dreams and aspirations? All of the foregoing is great and I have been doing it for years and I have accomplished most of my goals - I know others who have done all of the foregoing for years, but never accomplished anything, except create the next vision board – so what to do? Accomplish small goals, because they are worthy of celebration too. Don't go through every day thinking that you're a failure because you never realized your big goals. Turn that on its head and go through life as a raving success, because every day you're accomplishing your small goals – all of which will lead to the attainment of your big goals. Let me give you a few examples of the small things that I have done, and still do today – and every day. I write the first word of my new book, then a paragraph, then a chapter, and keep on keep on keeping on, until it's finished. Many of my books have been best-sellers, both non-fiction and fiction. I practice the first line of a speech that I am going to deliver in years-time, and I practice it over and over again. Many times I steal the limelight, get invited back and I have been written up as, "Britain's leading motivational speaker…". I make one phone call. Many times my phone calls invoke massive chain reactions, that have led to overwhelming success for me or my clients – many of whom have become millionaires. I sponsor one person and teach and train them to do the *correct* things *properly*. I am at the top of a massive MLM network. I celebrate each tiny success, in the full knowledge that acorns do turn into oak trees – particularly if they are nurtured. Cards on the table, for me, doing the small things that lead to BIG success, is far more important than creating the next vision board – no matter how evocative it is.

I QUIT MYTH #18 I find it too difficult to make money

Remedy: This superficial reason is very common and equally unnecessary. If the sponsor had properly educated the rep from day one; that this may turn out to be a slow-burn business, he could probably have arranged alternative finance to get him through the start-up period. We have already discussed how this business needs a critical mass before the real money comes in and that it takes a certain period of time to gain the skillsets that are necessary to build a team. Stick with it, allow an intelligent time frame, sufficient to do whatever it takes, to gain traction. The reason why most folk join an MLM opportunity is to make money, therefore it is imperative that all the upline should do 'every *single* thing' within their power to help each newbie rep start making money in quickest and most expedient manner.

I QUIT MYTH #19 My girlfriend does not support me.

Remedy. Sometimes life isn't fair and our partners do not support us in everything that we do. You have various options; you can persuade her to support and join you, you can sign her into the business, you can go it alone or you can find another partner. I really do believe this is an exciting life-style business that you can operate at any time to suit yourself, in practically any country in the world. For that reason alone, I think it's great if you can tie up with a partner who sees the business in an exciting light and also sees it as a lifestyle business that will afford to you financial independence; supercars, millionaire lifestyle, travel, vacations and holiday homes around the world – what more do you want?!

I QUIT MYTH #20 I want to do it all online or I want an online business

Remedy. These days with the internet, high speed broad band connection, and modern communications, even for an old timer like me it is an unadulterated pleasure using modern tools. There is just no excuse, because these days more and more business is being done online and what's more, done properly and professionally. Generally speaking I find that people fall into one of two camps. There will always be those willing to pay the price of learning, studying, practicing, evaluating and doing their own thinking and doing whatever it takes to get the job done. Creating success on the internet usually involves huge tracts of time going through a steep learning curve, working into the wee small hours, concentrated effort, no end of experimentation that you must diligently monitor, spending money on testing umpteen different things and driving traffic. Over and above everything else, do your own thinking and don't buy into all the guff and hyperbole that assures you how easy internet marketing is; usually perpetuated by those selling expensive packages making wild claims about 100,000 hits in your first week, a Kindle #1 best seller in your second, and $1,000,000 in your bank account by your third. In answer to all that, I would simply say: if it sounds too good to be true - it probably is! If you want to create a business online do what Stephen and I do and use email and Skype, and we use other methods for lead generation and we build sensibly – in depth. As long as you monitor what you are doing and learn as you go, and you'll get there. In Wide 'N Deep #4 Click & Grow Rich, I will show you some very pragmatic approaches to helping you harness the internet and modern communications. The techniques are explained in detail, with no geek-speak or techie-stuff, and they will turn out to be genuine, wealth-creating and life-changing tools for you, that will give you the lifestyle that you deserve.

I QUIT MYTH #21 My butt hurts. My parrot ate its foot. The car dropped. I'm broke. The TV caught fire. I caught my wotsit in the zip. The computer won't fire up. The lawn needs mowing. The sky fell in. I got lost. Aunty died of gangrene. We're going into the witness protection program.

Over the years I have heard just about every excuse under that Sun as to why people quit and it was one of those preposterous excuses that got me really thinking beyond all the superficial reasons, and hence the writing of this book. What really did it for me was when a guy phoned said, "I changed the lock on my front door and now I can't get out and I just hate it when that happens, but now I need to get out to clean the hamster who is covered in mud, because he's been playing with the pigs. The other thing I wanted to mention is that you're so smart, you make me feel stupid – so I quit!" You couldn't make it up. In a way, it did me a big favour, because it got my brain work furiously to vault way beyond all the superficial reasons and discover the one real reason why people quit MLM.

QUITTERS NEVER WIN, AND WINNERS NEVER QUIT

I love the story from the guy who decided to take up golf as a hobby and invested in a set of Honma Five Star clubs, bought all the expensive designer kit and started out, in good faith, to try and play golf. After a few weeks of trying very hard, he never really managed to hit the ball very far and certainly not on the right direction. What really brought his expensive foray to an abrupt end was the last two outings were at 7am on frost-cracking mornings, so he quit, and he made a *point* of telling me that he didn't *fail* – he *quit*. Now here's the thing: I don't think we should get hung up on semantics, because I don't think that will help us here. To my mind, either way, it just does not matter, because I don't think any of the folk in the previous examples are at fault or whether they quit or failed, is material. However, as leaders; uplines, networks, MLM companies and as an industry as a whole, I do believe that *we* are letting a lot of folk down and I believe all the myths that I have cited previously, are just superficial reasons as to why people quit our fabulous industry. The one thing that jumps off the page at me screaming is this: in most instances uplines are doing only a *bare minimum* of what they should and could be doing, to induce folk to *stick* with it. Lurking behind all that, are the MLM companies and they too could do more to induce people to *stick* with it – a whole lot more. I sincerely believe that more than a 1000% could be done to help; inspire, train, motivate, teach correct information and show reps how to make money and *stick* with us. Like all the folk who believed the Earth was flat, time has now come to allow the scales to fall from our eyes, and confront the truth that has been staring us in the face for an inordinate amount of time - let's explore why.

PART FOUR

WORKING IN DEPTH

Alan Turing, Algorithms and Network Marketing
It would be a reasonable question to ask; where on earth does Alan Turing and algorithms fit into the world of network marketing and who the hell is Alan Turing anyway? Alan Turing's story you may recall, has recently come to prominence in the blockbuster film, '*Imitation Games*' and I wrote a best seller called, *The Eureka! Enigma* in 2009 which featured him heavily, which is all about getting your brain to operate at optimum, come up with million dollar ideas and turn them into hard cash. Incidentally, the title of my book has recently been changed to *Millionaire Secrets - How to be a Millionaire*. Alan Turing's claim to fame, is that the during the second world war, he smashed the 'unbreakable' Enigma code. You may also recall another film called *Enigma* starring Kate Winslet, featuring a German U-boat whereby the Enigma code book was found. Of course the U-boats were

causing havoc by sinking merchant ships and by breaking the code, Turing's team was able direct allied warships to the area, and then destroy German U-boats with powerful depth charges. All of this was due to Turing's code breaking prowess and he is now, sixty years on, being recognized for his stupendous achievements in code breaking, computer sciences, mathematics and formalizing the use of algorithms which he used to break various codes, including Lorenz and the famed Enigma. His big idea was coming up with millions upon millions of non-solutions, in order clear the path to enable him to discover the ultimate solution. In creating his awesome algorithms to solve mind-numbing problems, Turing had to break down the problem into hundreds of individual components that could be conceptualized, visualized and assimilated. In the same vein we need to address the ginormous problems and complexities of network marketing in exactly the same way, and that's exactly what we are doing here. But before we do that, an interesting titbit: Alan was an avid collector of silver and apparently he had quite stash of coins and bullion bars that he secretly buried in the grounds of Bletchley Park in 1944, but he unfortunately forgot the location of his secret hiding place. Even as late as 2007, when I worked at Bletchley Park advising Tony Sale on a fundraising project, there were rumours floating around, about people with high-powered metal detectors scanning the grounds after dark – no one has admitted to finding anything - yet!

DEPTH CHARGE #1 We use many non-solutions to discover the solution

In the previous chapter we discussed a number of reasons why folk quit MLM and I deliberately labelled these as *superficial* reasons. In effect, these are the non-solutions that everyone seems to be hung up on and talking about, but in their own way, are distracting us all from getting to the heart of the issue, the real truth. We needed to get to the bottom of why folk quit MLM, and what we can do to encourage them to *stick* with us and I think there is a lot of potential to realize. By addressing all the non-solutions, the real cause of why people quit automatically appears – as if by magic, because it's been there all along. There are powerful forces at play here, and now they will be revealed to you.

DEPTH CHARGE #2 The starting point and the end point of working in depth is relatively simple to comprehend

When we start to talk about working in depth in the very early days of building a network, it is usually quite straight forward, relatively simple and fairly easy to grasp. It's only as we progress up the ladder, grey areas creep in and sometimes it begins to get complicated, sophisticated and even controversial. It's easy enough to see, that when you sign-up a new rep, you have to teach and train him, show him the ropes of how to list build; make phone calls, invite prospects to meetings, sponsor, sell products and then get him to teach and train *his* new recruit to do exactly the same thing. This is the beginning of the duplication process, where you are already, many times unwittingly, working in depth, albeit only one or two deep, but this the very *essence* of network marketing. Now let's jump right ahead to when you have built a massive team and you're not so much focused on sponsoring one-on-one, although this could definitely be part of it, but you're more concerned with working right in the depth of your network, and I really do mean right at the bottom of it as far as it goes. You do this in a totally different way to sponsoring your first rep, and this is what you need to aspire to. At the highest level, you work in depth by organizing and promoting large trainings and biz-opp meetings, having motivational rallies and events and talking to many, many prospects, reps and leaders all at the same time. Teaching, training and motivating the troops, and many times these may be outside of your immediate pay-line, but this quite acceptable, even encouraged, as we have previously touched upon, because they will be locking in distributors on your bottom line, which is where the really BIG money comes from.

DEPTH CHARGE #3 Leaders are leaders, but they are not usually networkers

Everyone realizes the key to growth is getting leaders, and the tried and tested formula is that they will come from the depth of your network. By definition, leaders have followers, and these will come in all shapes, forms, sizes and guises. The followers may by the congregation of a church; the members of a motorcycle, car, football or boat club, the audience of a pop-group or band or the loyal readers of a best-selling author, and the list goes on indefinitely, just use your imagination. The followers are all different, but what they all have in common, is that they adore their leader and more often than not, they will do whatever he says. For one reason or another, if he says, "It's a good idea to join this MLM," many of them will do so, very quickly and without question, and this alone illustrates the power of having a good rapport with folk. Massive growth will follow and everyone claps their hands. That is why you are looking for leaders and you should never forget this.

However, what happens next, is the classic way in which most networks have this famine and feast, of a massive spurt of growth, followed by stagnation, and shortly after the network begins to recede. What happens is this: A leader suddenly appears, as if by magic and invariably in the depth, and many times the upline are totally oblivious to this fact until they see some serious activity in their back office, or they hear through the grapevine that someone is sponsoring bucket loads of new reps. The usual response is that their mouths drop open and then they rub their hands together with glee and shout, "Wow, we have a leader and at least this leg is taking off!" Big mistake - Huge! What *many* of the upline *should* be saying is, "Wow, I have a leader on my hands, and I know that leaders are leaders, but they are not usually networkers. I hope someone has told already him that he *must not be too precious* with his people, because I must immediately get into the depth and establish a rapport with the new reps and teach and train them the power-of-one and that they should immediately be list building, pitching and recruiting one-on-one".

The more successful the leader is, the more exacerbated the problem becomes, because you will probably have more and more people who have not been taught and trained and properly; specifically that they must go out and recruit in the traditional way, one-on-one, until the next leader appears - as if magic in the depth. The salient point here is that all these followers, now new reps, be they 10, 30, 50, 100 or 500 in number, do not have a massive pool of followers to go at – they must find individuals they know personally, usually their own warm market. If upline leaders don't get into the depth below the new leader and start working with the newbies and teach and train them how to recruit and sponsor, the inevitable will happen: the network will begin to recede because the newbies are not locked in and have nothing happening for them. If you have legs that are continually receding and you have an untenable drop-out rate, you need to carefully consider what laws you are violating and correct it – because these laws are immutable. Remember, when the water recedes, we get to see who is swimming naked and it's usually people in the upline who never bothered to get into the depth of their network and teach and train the power-of-one; further, they are usually patting each other on the back, congratulating themselves as they go over the precipice like Lemmings, usually taking a large number of their downline with them. You see; every Tom, Dick or Harry thinks he knows, but he's WRONG! Having a successful leader just exacerbates the problem of having more and more people not being locked in and the whole thing becomes more and more inefficient, working in direct violation of Law #16: that if you don't lock people IN they drop OUT. If violating this law was a criminal offence, then half the network marketing population would be in jail. A quick footnote: in the fullness of time many of these schematics that I am talking you through now will soon be on YouTube videos and seeing me draw them up on a flip-chart will really help you visualize these important concepts. Make sure that you download *Turbo Success*, because that will get you onto my mailing list and very soon I will make contact with you and tell you where to view these life-changing videos. By the way, *Turbo Success* is one of the most powerful mind power books that you will ever read, and it's also FREE! www.TurboSuccess.com

DEPTH CHARGE #4 People with a large sphere of influence are often leaders, but many times they don't even know it

People like doctors; policeman, dentists, councilors, lawyers, firemen and many other professionals often have a sphere of influence that is very large, but many times these people are humble and self-effacing and don't even realize that large parts of the community look up to them. They could be super leaders for your team and just need drawing out and inviting in. Have your wits about yourself as you prospect, because many times these folk will be on 'chicken lists' because other MLMers are too timid to approach them, but like everyone else, they *may* be looking for ways to increase their disposable income.

DEPTH CHARGE #5 I'm going to keep going wider, more profit you see

I have just been thumbing through my Thesaurus trying hard to find a more fitting and more powerful word than 'asinine' but can't, so I'll stick with it. The other day I heard an 'asinine' conversation along the lines of: "I want to keep up everyone up close to me because I'm building for profit. As soon as I get a leg to Gold or diamond or whatever it is, I start a new leg, and instead of adhering to the companies recommended three legs, I'll have maybe five or perhaps ten legs. Keep up it all up close and personal, and in that way I get all the profit and it doesn't go to the company. And as I sponsor more and more reps personally, those people are not needed in the other legs, so they may as well go into new leg." Working in depth is all about utilizing the resource of human capital in an optimal way. To illustrate this we need a simple schematic, so let's take a person who wants to keep all the network up close and personal and then examine the outcome. To keep things simple, let's say this networker builds a simple network that is three wide and three deep. So on the front line you have three people, next level you have nine people and third level you'll have twenty seven people. It's ever so easy to see in this simple example, thirteen people are locked in and have at least one rep below them, so draw this out now, and convince yourself. Now let's say this same person, instead of driving the depth of his network says, "I want to keep everyone up close to me because I'm building for profit", so they start to build the same again with another leg. Let's say they do this five times with total of two hundred people, you will quickly see that the maximum amount of people you can lock in is sixty – all the rest are on the bottom line, completely vulnerable and not locked in, by virtue of the fact they have not a single person below them. And from here on in, it gets worse, simply because this erroneous methodology will get duplicated, and the next guy will want to do the same, but in his own way. He will want even more *profit,* and therefore quickly come to the erroneous conclusion that instead of five legs you need ten – all up close and personal and the next guy will duplicate this but with a variation on the theme and he will want twenty legs on his front line – more profit, get it? The guy after him; 'monkey see - monkey do' remember, will want 50-100 legs, even more profit – right? The real reason why the original conversation was 'asinine' was that he was talking about going wider, when his original legs were receding! What he should have been doing, is focusing all his mental and physical energy working in depth below the leaders and driving the depth in the legs he already had, teaching and training his reps the power-of-one, and locking people in below the leaders. If you build incorrectly, it will get duplicated and the drop-out rate will double, and also bear in mind that re-inventing the wheel for the majority of networkers is a full time occupation. History repeats itself, and once the decline has started, and a network begins to recede, it is nigh on impossible to stop it. I am convinced that you are already ahead of me, but if you structured those same two hundred folk all in a network three wide, and drove the depth, you would lock in over one hundred and twenty people. That's that same amount of resource, but double the lock in rate and that's awesome, and that's also how to make BIG money in network marketing. This is how it works, and as I have said it before, and I'll say it again; if you're missing this bit, you're not just missing PART of it, you're missing ALL of it and that's yet another major reason why they call MLM a thinking man's business.

DEPTH CHARGE #6 The black art of retention and working in depth

Over the years, I have heard many people say, particularly those that have quit network marketing, "Of course MLM is not a business that you can control, because you are dealing with people, and you are always waiting on others to do something - and most of them don't." They have completely missed the entire point. Working in depth allows you to overcome that major hurdle, and a whole load more beside. Working in depth is the 'Holy Grail' of network marketing, so please take this on board. It is the key to the City and the road map to the 'BIG money Jackpot' of MLM. By working in depth you'll have a business you can totally fly with, have complete control over, and grow your own MLM business, at your own pace.

We have already talked about network marketing being a warm market business and we talked about when you sign up a new rep you immediately start working closely with them. In turn, they will warmly introduce you to their people and very quickly those people will *warmly* introduce you to their people and suddenly you find yourself six, ten deep and you are driving that depth.

Working in depth is completely automatic and the least line of resistance, because it goes with the natural flow of things when it comes to building your network, whereas driving your width can frequently be an altogether slower proposition.

Steven Harris and I spend fifty percent of our time finding new reps to sign up and we place those new reps in the depth, as we strategically lock people in, and simultaneously work with those who are already in our depth. Generally speaking you want to keep the width as narrow as you can on your front-line, in keeping with making your own MLM compensation plan work optimally. Obviously talk to your upline to get their understanding and wisdom on this, but in principle, the narrower your front line and deeper in depth, the better. Stephen and I say, "Drive depth, if you want a pension for life."

DEPTH CHARGE #7 Has the penny dropped yet?

You may already be experiencing an epiphany moment about the real reason why folk *stick* with MLM, as opposed to all the superficial reasons why people quit. My contention is that if lots of folk are working and driving depth and locking people in properly, the retention rate would increase dramatically, because new reps would quickly have others below them, their businesses would be flying and they would be making money - there would be no reason to leave. Perhaps for you, more evidence is required.

DEPTH CHARGE #8 Let's fill in some gaps

This is where it begins to get complicated, because there is so much to go at it, that it's quite difficult to set a chronology that makes sense of it all. Like a lot of this material, it needs to be read over and over again, and not just read, but *studied* and assimilated. My starting point is this; when you sign your first rep you must take the time to *adequately explain*, in your own words, that you will be helping him get people on board, from both your warm market and particularly his warm market and helping him build his downlines, and to do this you will be working very closely with all those people, both his and yours. Big mistakes are made right here, in the very early days, by newbies and seasoned pros alike. By the way, telling your new reps the foregoing isn't optional it's obligatory, for many reasons, including this one. Recall the 80-20 law that only 20% of the people will do all the work and sales. Bearing this in mind, you never really know who will do what and the odds are not stacked in your favour of finding a 'networker' as opposed to finding a 'notworker'. Therefore you must establish a proper rapport with the reps in your depth to and ensure that they are being properly taught and trained and that you have all their contact details just in case their leader or sponsor, for one reason or another, doesn't work out, or quits.

DEPTH CHARGE #9 Grasp the magic principles sooner rather than later

The first point about working in depth is to grasp the principle that you work very closely with the reps that you bring into your business and then immediately work very closely with the people they bring into the business, and then teach and train them the same thing. I now want you to stop this audio or stop reading the book and grab a sheet of paper and draw a circle on it. Write in that circle, 'You' or your own name and then underneath it, draw fifteen other circles *horizontally* and link them individually to you. Name those fifteen circles, John, David, Paul, Sally or choose names that you like. Ostensibly, all these people are on your front line, all connected to you. Have a close look at that network. There is nobody locked in other than you. In other words, out of those fifteen people not a single one of them has anyone underneath them, in their network. You have fifteen people, all in your network, but they are all vulnerable. Not a single rep has got any excitement or enthusiasm; none of them has a business, not even a small one. You may have fifteen people on your front line, but it is not going to do you any good. I have witnessed it many times, whereby reps sponsor a lot of distributors on their front line and over time, one by one they drop out of the business. Now what I want you to do, is draw another circle and again write in it, 'You' or your own name, and then draw fifteen other circles in a *vertical* line below you, all linked to each other. Now here's the thing: I am not telling you this is the way to build your business, but what I am giving you is powerful lesson in working in depth, and locking people into a network. This is by way of an example only. You may call this methodology *'stacking'* if you like, and it's very powerful. If you study your drawing, you will quickly see that there is only one person who is *not* excited and that is the guy at the very bottom. All the others are locked in and have at least one person in their depth. Now that's exciting! If you have eight or ten people in your depth, that's not just plain exciting, that's epic! What we are talking about here is utilizing the resource, the human capital, to its optimum advantage.

DEPTH CHARGE #10 The level of feeling is a motivator – for everyone

Before we move away from the example outlined above, let's examine it a little more closely to enable you to get a real handle on it. I want you to really start experiencing your innermost feelings here, and very quickly you'll get the jist of it. Let's imagine that you are at the bottom of the stack and you are not locked in. What are your thoughts and how do you feel? This is depressing place to be, you have no one in your business, you are all dressed up and no place to go. You've got it all to do and you *feel vulnerable*. Let's hope your upline comes to the rescue and teaches and trains you and helps you get your first rep on board.

Now move yourself up just one notch, to the level above, and note how you feel now. Well you've got your first rep on board and you've started your MLM business. Wow - that's fantastic! This is so important let's hope your upline recognize this and awards you with a pin, presents you with a certificate, takes you to lunch, cheers you from the stage, takes you to dinner, buys you donuts, gives you a big clap on the back and encourages you to go out and find your next one. Now let jump up five notches, so you now have seven people below you. That's quite a team and you are becoming quite a good leader and motivator; you should *feel incredible*, pat yourself on the back and start pulling your team together, ramp up pep-talks, the teaching, training and assisting them. Life has never been better, you're heading in the right direction. Now jump seven notches up and you're right up the top of the leg where we started from. You now have fourteen people below, all locked in except the guy at the bottom, and you're heading toward having a critical mass. You *feel invincible*, and you need to be thinking strategically to capitalize on your great success. In all possibility, you need to be thinking about starting and driving another leg to balance things out, to reach your commission levels.

You'll be thinking strategically about every rep in your team, about you how you can best serve them, motivate them, inspire them, turn them into leaders and help them accomplish their next level. I suggest that you carry out this exercise even more thoroughly, and write out short paragraphs denoting *each* of the *fourteen* levels in the downline. How do you *feel* at each and every level, what you need to be doing action-wise at each level and when comes to giving pep talks and advice to the people in your depth, how you handle each rep in an individual manner, because each one of them will be experiencing totally different *feelings* - in accordance to how many reps they may or may not have in their depth?

DEPTH CHARGE #11 Width equals vulnerability and depth equals security

I can almost hear you say, "But we were told that width equals profitability and depth equals security, so what's going on?" The truth is, you only got half the story, which frequently happens. Width in your depth does equal profitably, but not the width on your front line. Let's examine a network that is three wide and pays eight levels deep and it pays residual $6 a month for each person in the network. If this is not a fixed matrix, it most certainly will not fill up uniformly, but for our exercise, let's assume it does, to illustrate the point. If we have three reps on the front line the pay out there is $18 a month. But the bottom level will have circa 6000 reps on it, and that equates to $36,000 a month and don't forget in addition, you'll be picking up all the levels above that, including the $18 from your front line. The vulnerability comes from driving too wide on your frontline, because getting enough people in through the front door quicker than they leave through the back door is real problem, and the *main* reason why people quit MLM. Even seasoned MLMers make the mistake referring to width as front line only, but this completely wrong, because it distracts us and forces us to take our eye off the ball, as to where the real mother-lode is, which of course in the width of the network, including all levels, but especially the bottom level and beyond where all the good work of locking in is done - to ensure your pension for life. While we are still on the subject, of 'width equals profitability', I think we needed to squeeze the spot and examine the saying, just to take the ambiguity out of it, because it's counter-productive to teach and train things that are ambiguous.

DEPTH CHARGE #12 When there is a sign-up in depth, the entire upline get excited

By signing up reps in the depth of your network you create a massive buzz because every single rep in the upline gets excited. We call this lighting the fire in the depth and it's something you need to take advantage of. You do this by making sure that every single rep in the line is aware of the new rep signing up and this activity is what creates the buzz. If your team doesn't make the phone calls or send texts and create the awareness, a tremendous amount of amount of leverage and buzz is lost. As you spot leaders in depth it is also imperative that everyone in the upline gets know to about it, further fanning the flames of motivation and increasing action.

DEPTH CHARGE #13 One leads to one, who leads to one, who leads to a leader

This industry is full of amazing twists, turns, black holes, rabbit holes, rabbit ears, and other conundrums. This is one of my favorites and the more reps that begin to understand it the better. It starts with grasping the cold hard fact that leaders come from the depth and this strategy is *eminently duplicatable*, teachable and trainable, whereas getting leaders on your front line is *most definitely not*. The second part, is that it is very difficult to qualify who will actually fly in this business or not and the third part is that even if you did qualify people superbly, you still have absolutely no control or say in the matter, over who the people in your depth may sponsor. In fact, I guarantee that you will be in for one or two surprises and even the occasional shock. The point is this: what you really need to be doing is sponsoring hard and building depth and encouraging all your reps to do the same. Invariably what happens is that one passive will sign one rep who signs another passive rep, who signs another passive rep, who ultimately signs a leader. Now this leader may come from the second, third, fourth, or even eighth level, and when he does appear, embrace him, and begin to work with his people in the depth by teaching and training them. When you set the fire in the basement and work upward from there, you will frequently be amazed as to how many passives in the upline will suddenly thaw out because of the heat and come to life. As Stephen and I say: when there is a rock star in the basement, make sure everyone hears the noise.

DEPTH CHARGE #14 Why we happily work outside our pay-line

Let's assume that you now have a massive line on the your bottom of your network, of say 6000 reps who all vulnerable, and for illustrative purposes, let's say they are not yet locked in. In other words it's a massive width, but no depth below them. You can easily see that this is the most lucrative part of your network, and that is why you have been diligently driving depth. Big well done! This is where the BIG money comes from, and if you want an unrivalled pension fund for life, you must drive those legs way beyond your own pay-line. At any one time, Steven Harris and I have somewhere between 50-75% of our business *outside* our immediate pay line which is eight levels deep. In many MLMs there are usually bonuses whereby, when you have reached certain levels, you can pick up a small commission on everyone who is in your network, even those outside your payline, but usually with some provisos.

DEPTH CHARGE #15 Listen to these audios until the plan takes root at a cellular level in your own brain

Here is an little interesting snippet: when we pushed my Talk & Grow Rich audios out there in a big way we sold hundreds of thousands of them and we conducted a survey on many of the people who had bought them and subsequently filled in the attached questionnaire. We wanted to know how many times that our customers listened to the audios; and we were blown away, because it was an average of thirty times, because they would put the cassette into the player in their car and listen to it over and over again. I expect this Wide 'N Deep series to be listened to fifty to a hundred times, perhaps more, because there is so much here about working in depth that needs to be heard over and over again, if you are to get into the big money in MLM. So listen to these audios until the penny drops and you go, Wow! – At last I know what I've got to do!

DEPTH CHARGE #16 Practice drawing circles 'til the penny drops

Throughout this program, I hope I have made it clear that you should draw those schematic circles over and over again, so that you can see with your own eyes what the real difference is between driving width and driving depth. Make sure you see all my schematics on YouTube and get a Free copy of *Turbo Success* at www.TurboSuccess.com and get on my mailing list for updates. The other point I want to be crystal clear about is this: I am not talking about fixed matrixes, binary plans, stacking or any other MLM methodology. What am talking about is the most effective use of the resource in any network, its human capital. Of course I understand that there are as many MLM compensation plans as there are accountants, and many MLM companies may insist that you drive 6,12 or 18 legs, but here I am using a three wide – eight deep plan to illustrate the difference between working in width and working in depth, so if anyone says to you, "Well, we don't believe in stacking, or that won't work in our network." They have obviously missed the whole point and you need to tell them to start at the beginning of the book again, and keep reading it, until the really penny drops, and at the same time perhaps you should check to see whether they think the World is flat, the Sun travels around the Earth and that the World is only 6000 years old.

DEPTH CHARGE #17 An astounding illustration of exponential growth

I want to reiterate a simple story that I think illustrates exponential growth admirably. The story is about a job opportunity that we used earlier in this book, but this time around I think it might make a whole bunch more sense to you: There are two job packages available. The first one is $30,000 a month for 30 days and the other package is $2.00 a day, which doubles up every day for 30 days. Which package would you take? I guarantee most people take $30,000 for 30 days because they soon work out that $1,000 a day is good money and at the same time they just cannot perceive how $2.00 a day doubling up, could equal or overtake that. But let's fly through this and have a quick look at it, and then let us examine how this equates to building a network. This time around I think you will grasp the real power of this silly exercise, so here goes: Day one you get $2 and that doubles every day: $4, $8, $16, $32, $64. Let's just round it off to $125 to make the figures simple and then double up again to $250, $500, $1000, $2,000, $4,000, $8,000, $16,000, $32,000, $64,000 round it up $125,000 just to make the figures easy. Doubling up again $125,000 turns into $250,000 turns into $500,000 and that doubles into 1 million, 2 million, 4 million, 8 million, 16 million, 32 million, 64 million. Day 27 let us round it up again 125 million doubles up again 250 million, then 500 million, which is half a billion and the final day 500 million and turns into a billion dollars. Then add all the last 30 days income together, and that brings you to a grand total of over 2 billion dollars – which is absolutely staggering.

DEPTH CHARGE #18 Exploring the exponential growth of human capital

Now I want to talk about human capital and building your network. For this exercise, let's assume that you are building a network three wide and you are teaching each of those people how to find and recruit three people each; very quickly you are going to gain a critical mass and you are going to have ten people in your network. It's very important for you to know, that these ten people are not *ordinary* people, but folk that have been taught and trained in the power-of-one. Those ten people will find one person each for their group, and that is going to turn your group into a network of twenty people. Again, not twenty *ordinary* people, because that alone would not work; these people have to be *specifically* taught and trained in the power-of-one, of how to recruit one person into their network, and teach and train that rep to do exactly the same thing. You see it's all about teaching and training people, how to find one, recruit one and then help that person find one and recruit one, because as those twenty people double up, they will find one person each and suddenly you have got forty people, not *ordinary* people but people who have been *diligently* taught and trained. This is a teaching and training business; and forty people who will soon find one person each, and in the shortest space of time, you have eighty people in your network. Even the largest networks are built one person at a time, and in this manner Stephen Harris and I have a massive network that spans the globe. Taking on board correct information, about how networks grow, and if you encourage everyone in your network to take that on board, this thing will come together for you very quickly. There will be no treading on peanut butter or hanging around slow growth, because the relentless use of the power-of-one will create exponential growth for you – and that's life in the fast lane, and the fast lane is where you want to be right!? That's exciting! Say it with me, "That's exiting!" – fantastic!

DEPTH CHARGE #19 Passives can do a whole load of work, if you play your cards right

Leaders and upliners must become much more sophisticated in the way they build their networks and stop the abusive use of human capital. Many times they are totally oblivious of the massive power of 'orphans' and 'passives' which will at any one time will amount to 80% of their network. Passives are usually viewed as those who do little or no work; sponsoring or buyer or selling of products, other than purchasing their minimum monthly quota. To all intents and purposes they sit there passively doing nothing, but this is totally the wrong way of viewing it. Even if passives do no 'actual' work they can be accomplishing *meaningful results* if they were positioned correctly in the network, locking in those above them. This is the 'key to the kingdom' and more often than not, it is completely missed. Of course I am aware that each and every company has its rules and regulations of how you can place, stack and move reps, passives and orphans. But I am talking about an industry epidemic of poor retention, and some companies themselves may have to look at the way they have inadvertently created inefficient structures, offerings and incentives for building them. If you were to ask me how many companies have structures that could be improved upon I would say, of the ones I have looked at, and that's plenty, about ninety-five percent are not operating optimally - and that's being kind!

DEPTH CHARGE #20 I will help you build one leg

You can even say to a rep, "I will drive one leg and you drive the other." In this way you don't end up doing all the work, but it usually motivates others into working hard as well. This is great in theory and Stephen and I use it all the time in practice too. It means that we can drive a power leg, just by driving depth and many times you can gain tremendous momentum, if you can get enough people running with it. But what happens when you are driving the power leg and the other leg that the rep is supposed to be driving, isn't keeping up with you, and he needs more reps or volume to qualify to his next level? You could say,

'Well we've done enough, if he wants to make money, he'll have to build the other leg himself,' or do you jump into the weak leg and help him with that too, and in effect you end up doing all or most of the work yourself? The truth is, each situation needs to be addressed as it arises and sometimes you can look around your network and see that by helping someone else, you can kill two birds with one stone. One thing is for sure, that in this business if you leave people to their own devices you can be waiting for a long time and sometimes it pays to help people accomplish their goals, by doing whatever it takes – whether they are ready or not. By helping enough others accomplish their goals, our goals are self-assured, is another one of MLMs big paradoxes, that you will need to embrace - sooner rather than later.

DEPTH CHARGE #21 Why passives will inherit the earth

It's worthy of lots of thought because every single network, including yours, is subject to immutable laws and it is inevitable that each network will end up with 80% of people who are passive and not doing any of the real work in terms of massive recruiting or selling huge volumes of product. But let's turn this on its head and instead of violating the law, let's harness the law. Instead of saying, 'the majority of the network are not doing any of the work' let's view it like this: The 'passives' are always the 80% and are the bulk of what we have, and without them there wouldn't be a network of any substance. And in many instances, either directly or indirectly, we find the leaders through the passives; because one leads to one, who leads to one who leads to a leader. In other words the passives, which are the bulk of the network, are the *magic cement* that glue the whole thing together. That's a big 'Wow!' right there! Further, you can view the 'passives' as doing a huge amount of work, just be being there, locking others into place. That's another big Wow! – you'd better believe it. I am minded of the times that I have seen someone join an MLM and they only sponsored one person in four months, so they convinced themselves, "this is no good, it's not working." The one person they sponsored went on to make a million bucks. I have seen this not just once, but a few times. Think about it, and don't give up too quickly.

DEPTH CHARGE #22 A team that drives depth together, stays together

If leaders who are driving the business sponsor more reps than they need on their own front line, the most efficient place for them to go is in the depth of the network, not building yet another weak leg, which only exacerbates the problem. There are a number of problems associated with this, all of which can, with a little forethought, be overcome. The first is, that if you sponsor someone, then place them in the depth, they must have it explained to them, that they can still work directly with you. They should also be encouraged to work directly with their new sponsor or link, and develop a strong personal relationship with that person. Adopt this attitude of working together and develop one big happy family, because even if they don't actually know this person, they can still become friends, establish a rapport and start working together – as a team.

DEPTH CHARGE #23 The difference between controllable and un-controllable is only two small letters - but they make the difference between colossal success and lugubrious failure

So many folk erroneously believe that MLM is not a controllable business because you are always relying on other people, and if those reps don't recruit, build and sell products, with that kind of erroneous belief system, of course you're going to have a massive problem on your hands. Driving depth overcomes that issue admirably, because you are continually working with people and circumventing anyone who is not teaching training or working at your pace or for any other reason at all. Most important of all, is that you continually taking the initiative to get into the depth of your network and teach and train everyone about the power-of-one and of course diligently collect names; addresses, emails and telephone numbers of the people in your network, no matter who brought them in. These are a few of the things that winners do, and the others don't. When my mentor Gibbs was teaching me, he *insisted* that I write down the following sentence at least a hundred times, and I did: Working in depth is the ONE and ONLY tool that ensures MLM can be a controllable business.

DEPTH CHARGE #24 What's your version of ham and beans

This exciting industry of ours has so much going for it and one of the things that I particularly love and embrace, is the fact that it is a lifestyle business. That means you should be taking advantage of the fact, and turning sizzle sessions and training meetings into exciting and meaningful events and even though they may small, you can still do this by asking people to bring a covered plate or some kind of food contribution. You could announce that it's a, 'Ham 'N Beans' meeting and let it be known to your group to bring either some ham or beans, French sticks or a tin of biscuits or box of crackers. Encourage your team to bring the tastiest plate they can, in the nicest dish that they can lay their hands on, along with the best butter, mayonnaise, chips, soft drinks and napkins. Why? Because this is lifestyle business and you want your event to be memorable for the right reasons; and nice food, for most people, is a major part lifestyle. The whole idea is to make your event a great two hour or five hour training or even a full day event, and create an ambience, buzz bonding and comradery amongst the whole team. If you get this right, you'll have folk with their tongues hanging out, eagerly anticipating your next event, which is going to be even better – and even more *productive*, right!?

DEPTH CHARGE #25 Pros come to life the first day of the month - the rest come to life on the 25th of the month

There is strange phenomenon that sweeps across the network marketing industry on the 25th of every month and that is when every rep wakes up to the fact that they haven't qualified. They suddenly get their skates on and pull out all the stops; recruit, sell product and encourage their team to do the same as though their very lives depended upon it. However, the pros don't do this. The Pros are 'in the zone' day one of the month and they stay 'in the zone' until the last day of the month and then they start again, 'in the zone', on the first of the month. Pros start the month, absolutely knowing that they will qualify, and work hard every day at building their network and aim to make it their best month ever. That's why they're pros, and the rest of the field just qualify by the skin on their teeth.

DEPTH CHARGE #26 Bring your network to life - with a flip chart

Even in the very early days of starting a network, I am a great believer in having a large paper flip chart, on a tripod in my office, where I can draw out circles of my growing network. Even if there is no one there to start with, I can draw up circles of what I want the network to look like and put in fictitious names. For me it is impossible to work out a strategy without visuals, and having a flip chart allows you to address members of your group virtually, even if they are not physically present and ask them what it is they would like help with. I often am surprised that by talking to the flip chart, my mind is suddenly charged with ideas and I know exactly what each member of my group needs in the way of advice; an empowering pep talk, direction, structuring, personal problems or something else. I know many of my younger team members prefer to draw out their circles on computer screen, but to me there is something magical about having a paper flip chart. It also lends itself to drawing up circles for presenting to prospects and reps alike when they come to my office, and I guess we get through two or three flip chart pads a week, which I consider to be an *investment*, not just money well spent. Magic moments and happy days!

DEPTH CHARGE #27 Dream building, goal setting, mind power work and visualization are paramount
Whenever you are surrounded by a team, that resource will be in constant need of motivation, stimulation, encouragement and leadership – and coffee and biscuits. One of the most powerful things you can and must do on a consistent basis, is teach people how to harness their neck-top computer, the billion dollar biocomputer, which is their own brain - and dream big. You need to encourage them to develop their own dreams, goals and aspirations and not foist your goals on them. Encourage them to link their goals to a plan of action, of how they will attain those goals, by linking them to certain achievable steps within the business. Urge your reps to take on board that they already have all the resources they require to succeed – and that resource is between their ears. My international best-seller, *Turbo Success – How to Reprogram the Human Biocomputer* is one of the most powerful mind power books ever written, and is all about programming your mind for success, and you can get your FREE copy

here: www.TurboSuccess.com and feel free to give the link to your friends too. If your friends like the book as much as you do, perhaps these friends can be the beginning of your own mastermind group.

DEPTH CHARGE #28 Successful leaders intuitively understand the MLM paradoxes

Attaining success in any industry can frequently be counter intuitive, but I would say this is more true in the MLM industry, more so than others. It pays to be constantly reminding yourself of the rules of the game, and what it is that the big boys do. Working in depth, particularly outside of your pay-line just doesn't sound right, but it is. If you help enough other people get what they want, your own goals are self-assured, just doesn't sound right, particularly when in most corporate structures the only person you need to be thinking about is #1 – but again this is right. Going into no-mind for a daily meditation routine when you stop thinking and hand all your problems to your subconscious mind, when you probably think you should be trying to solve your problems consciously, just doesn't scan for most people, but you should try it sometime – because there is no other way.

DEPTH CHARGE #29 Help them to qualify and accomplish their goal, whether they are ready or not

This business is *driven* and for you to succeed and get into the BIG money you must *drive* it hard. I see so many people timidly coaxing their reps along and usually getting very frustrated in the process, because nothing seems to be happening quick enough. The industry leaders don't do this. By working in depth and by constantly taking the initiative and working with the teams in each leg, you are in effect forcing those on your front line people and others in the team to get cracking, and keep up with your pace. Many times, if you leave reps to their own devices you're going to be there forever and in this business, you have don't forever – because everything good comes out of momentum. Remember also, the speed of the leader is the speed of the group, and money loves speed. This is what I call the greenhouse effect, and most reps need nurturing and growing, not with sunshine and water, but with teaching; training, showing and leading, and driving them hard to their next level - *whether they are ready or not* - and nine times out of ten, the won't be. To an outsider it may appear that you are doing all the work, but this is just one of those MLM paradoxes that you need to embrace.

By working in this fashion, invariably what will happen is that the front liner, or whoever else it is that you are working with, doesn't step up to the plate, someone with leadership qualities and initiative will, and because you're working down there in depth with them, you will immediately recognize them as a leader and help them reach their full potential. MLM is the best place to grow people and also see if their personal strategies for success are working out in the real world - because it will be patently obvious for them and also the rest of network and the big wide world to see, every single step of the way.

DEPTH CHARGE #30 Skyscrapers need deep foundations before they scrape the sky
Over the past forty years I have occasionally lived in Manhattan, the Big Apple, and periodically stayed in the Dakota where John Lennon lived, stayed many times at the prestigious Waldorf Astoria and certainly on more than one occasion, in the cheapest slop houses the city has to offer - ugh! One thing that has always fascinated me, is watching crater-size holes appear in the ground for what seems to be an inordinate period of time, as the foundations for a skyscraper being are excavated. What

happens next is equally mind blowing, and that is once the foundations are in place, how quickly the skyscraper goes up and opening day comes around. Sheer Magic! Every time I witness this phenomenon, I am minded about reps who approach the MLM industry in a naive manner. Perhaps no one has managed their expectations or on the contrary, maybe they have even encouraged to think that there is a likelihood they will earn a million bucks in their first week. A much better approach would be to manage a new reps expectations, and explain in detail about building foundations in the form of a critical mass, of say, ten to twenty people in the group, spending twelve to eighteen months gaining all the industry skills of list building, prospecting, closing and selling products; that are required to tap into the really BIG money that is available to those who build substantial networks and move serious volumes of product, and then spend three to five exciting, action packed years building a cash generative network. In other words, put the foundations in place first, and *then* watch your network grow exponentially, like a New York City skyscraper.

DEPTH CHARGE #31 Either way, people must talk to each other, and act as team

Of course all networks are different in the ways you can sign, sponsor and donate or place people in the depth. In our network you can leave people on your own front line for up to sixty days before you place them strategically in your network. The thinking behind this is that you can see how they perform in the holding tank period and if they are going to be a leader keep them up close and personal. Of course it's all down to preferences and I fully understand both sides of the argument. My preference is, bearing in mind the 80-20 rule, the odds are stacked against you in terms of finding a leader within sixty days. So my preference is to *immediately* place that person in the depth of the network, whereby I can guarantee that person will still do *magnificent* work - even if they do absolutely nothing. If you have signed a new rep, and then place that person in the depth under a complete stranger, at the very least try to get them to talk with each other and develop a rapport with that person who is above him, and if possible some more people in the upline too. In that way he can cultivate a proper relationship going forward and then gain help and assistance from other reps other than yourself.

The other way to do it is to get the person to the point of signing and then hand them over to the person you are going to place them under and let that rep sign them, as though it was his prospect.

DEPTH CHARGE #32 Time is a killer and momentum is a life saver

Let's talk a little more about driving depth as opposed to driving width. There is a huge difference and time alone can make you or break you. It's like this: When you're driving depth, as long as you are sponsoring and the people in the downline are sponsoring, the amount of activity in that leg will be enough to keep everyone motivated, locked in and moving along. The downward momentum is a life saver. Now that isn't what happens when you are building width and sponsoring on your front line. What usually happens is that as you sponsor in width and then move to another leg, and start the process again and again, no one is getting excited and the thinner you spread yourself with more and more legs, the more exacerbated the problem becomes. It is time, the days, weeks and months, that is the killer. For example if this was a computer game with no time involved working width, that would be fine if it was instantaneous. But time is a killer, and what happens is that as you go off and start another leg, time is ticking by for the first leg, where in all likelihood there is not too much action. Then you start another leg, and now time is ticking by for the first *and* the second leg, and so it goes on. No one gets excited, no one's business grows and as move across the width the first guy starts getting bored, not making money and can't see any prospect of growth, so he quits. It's like keeping melons down in a bath of water. You try to push one down over here and two others pop up over there. You'll be having people leave by the back door quicker than you can get them in through the front door. It's ninety percent easier to drive depth than width because everything including time *and* momentum, is working in your favour.

DEPTH CHARGE #33 Plugging reps into systems is crucial

As soon as reps sign into the business, it is crucial that they are plugged into all and any systems that you may have set up, to give them the best possible chance of taking all the intel on board; have access to trainings, three way calls, support, duplication, book of the month, webinars, and whatever else it is you may have. If you haven't got systems in place, now is the time to do so, and those reps who are already making big money in MLM, know that the more *correct* information that is made available using audio, video and printed materials, the more likely that each and every rep will replicate the same. In Wide 'N Deep #4 Click & Grow Rich we explore many ways of harnessing the Internet and modern communications and how to set up plug in systems that allow you communicate, motivate, teach, train, zap, zing, explode, crush and Rock 'N Roll, all at the same time – now that's not Magic, it's a Miracle!

DEPTH CHARGE #34 Make sure the correct message is still stuck to the baton when you hand it over

I like to think of MLM as a relay race, whereby you have a baton and a scroll tied to it with red ribbon, that you hand over to the next runner and he drives the race forward from there. In MLM, it is imperative that you hand the baton with the correct message stuck to it. The rules stuck on the baton categorically state: Keep driving depth until you get replicated by a leader who will take the baton *and* the instructions and keep driving depth whether it be three, five or eight down, *until* you get replicated perfectly. If you do this, your dropout rate will dramatically reduce and your network will stop receding. Once you have got properly replicated in a leg, you can then jump into another leg and start the process again. The penalties for violating Law #14 are severe; therefore it is imperative that you give quality time, to ensure that correct and meaningful things are duplicated.

DEPTH CHARGE #35 If it's not 100% right - it's 100% wrong

First and foremost, it is up the leaders in the field to band together and point out any flaws in the compensation plan if it is formulated wrongly from the company standpoint, forcing reps to place people in the wrong positions in the network, or does not position them optimally. Secondly, it is then up to the companies to grasp all the implications of the diabolical waste of human resource, and then aim to reduce the unacceptable churn rate by creating a plan that is attractive, retentive and drives and rewards for depth, not width, which masterfully and elegantly addresses this problem. Companies and network leaders could give a *lot* more thought, incentives and recognition for completing the most important job of all - and that is the signing of a first new rep. The reason why this job is so vitally important, is that 80% of the network being in the passive category, to move that forward by getting just one more rep on board is a mammoth step to getting nearer to finding a leader or someone who is at least pro-active - this simple act of signing-one, *guarantees* the *perpetuation* of your network. The incentive for completing this praiseworthy task doesn't have to be soleley monetary, it could be a pin, a certificate, a badge or applause from the stage – above everything, leaders in the field should know how *crucial* this one step is, and my feeling is that currently many of them don't, no matter how many times they hear; that one leads to one, leads to one, who ultimately leads to a leader.

DEPTH CHARGE #36 Close ranks on those who perpetuate myths

Every single individual rep can do his or her bit on helping to create a better industry for all. If you hear someone telling you or others to drive width instead of depth, without exceptionally good reason, you can and should close ranks on them and get to the bottom of what their agenda is, and ask for thorough explanations. Like so many people, maybe they don't understand and for them the penny still hasn't dropped, but regardless of that, I firmly believe that if enough people stand up for their rights, and try to make things better, the industry as a whole will turn a massive corner for the better – and never look back.

DEPTH CHARGE #37 We must stop wasting hundreds of millions of man hours

Our appalling industry churn rate results in hundreds of millions of man hours being wasted, having to go out and find and teach and train new people. It's demoralizing, destructive and totally unprofitable for companies and reps in the field alike. Network leaders and MLM company managers and owners must to stop buying into and perpetuating the myth that there has to be this untenable, colossal and unacceptable churn rate within our industry. It's simple not true – it just needs addressing professionally. It needs thinking about, organizing and more than anything a meeting of minds between the leaders in the field and managers of the MLM companies who are creating compensation plans that are causing a major part of the problem, primarily because they are violating too many immutable laws. The current problem is that there is generally a big communication gap between the leaders in the field and the managers who are running the MLM companies and both parties are usually in 'ostrich mode' or otherwise totally oblivious to the 'churn rate' problem.

DEPTH CHARGE #38 Success is a two way street

Don't assume the company has necessarily got the figures and compensation plan right. Over the decades, thousands of MLMs have gone down the gurgler, so they must have got something wrong. Often born out of ignorance and greed, the company may inadvertently be driving you to build width, which is neither expedient nor tenable and they are making a rod for your back - although it may be more profitable for them. They may be hanging you out to dry, and neither you nor them, may know it.

DEPTH CHARGE #39 The evidence is staring us in the face

The appalling drop-out rate in our industry is between 85% and 95%. I believe that it's nearer higher figure, but it is hard to ascertain, because you have to get past all the noise; much of which is probably perpetuated by folk in the industry, many of whom should know better. When you carefully consider immutable Law #16: If networkers are not locked IN, they will drop OUT, you must study how the figures work, and they work proportionally both ways. If you start more legs, the lock-in rate gets *proportionally worse* and if you build more depth the lock-in rate gets *proportionally better.* So you know what to do, and where you heard it first.

DEPTH CHARGE #40 Our industry is facing a crisis of epidemic proportions. Let's face it head on

Our industry is facing is a problem of the same magnitude that Formula One (F1) was facing in the 70s and 80s when drivers were getting killed on treacherous race circuits in dangerous race cars, at an unprecedented rate. It took a number of very brave drivers including; Jackie Stewart, Niki Lauda, Sterling Moss and Graham Hill to band together and talk to the track owners and force them into increasing safety measures at every level. Within a few short years, far fewer racing drivers were getting killed and these days although cars are a lot faster, the tracks and race cars are incredibly safe. What is needed in our industry is a team of MLM pros to band together as a mastermind group, and work out all the variables of creating compensation plans with a view to substantially enhancing retention and massively reducing drop out, then persuade the MLM companies that it is in their interest as well, to take on board and act upon the intel. What cannot go on is this merry-go-round, that frequently isn't so merry, of recruit; sponsor, teach, train and then have the same people quit, many times within weeks or a few months of joining, and then start the whole vicious cycle again. For deep-rooted cultural change you need a change in attitude by people who run the MLM industry - anyone can see that – surely!? I welcome the thoughts and ideas by other leaders from the field and management from MLM companies. The FI analogy that I have used is a pertinent one, because all the drivers were all competing against each other and were in different teams, but they came together in a spirit of unison, to fight powerful common cause. I believe our cause of substantially reducing the untenable churn rate of our industry is now at a crucial stage – and well worth fighting for.

DEPTH CHARGE # 41 MLM companies and the leaders in the field need to work more closely together

This is the time to re-evaluate what we are doing; as individual reps, as networks, as MLM companies and as the industry as whole. After hundreds of millions of hours in the field and after six decades, let's look closely at what we are doing wrong and correct it, and also what we are doing right and embrace it. There's been far too much smoke and mirrors, for far too long – now is the time to get back to pure magic. For far too long, those addressing the churn rate have been solely focused on the networks and the networkers, but the truth is, to create permanent change we really need to be focused on the networks, networkers *and* the MLM companies creating the compensation plans, simultaneously. We need to be thinking in terms of plans that work harmoniously with the immutable laws, bearing in mind all the time how to optimise retention and lock-in rate, every single step of the way. As an industry that is six decades old with an absolute terrible track record of churn we certainly have loads of stats and examples to go at and ways not to do it. What about all those that have dropped out, quit, gone quietly away? I am not taking about millions, I am talking about tens of millions of folk. Even if 80% of them were 'passives' would you like some of them in your downline? I'd take the lot – LOL. Network leaders shouldn't accept the status quo, because doing it wrong, is all too much like hard work, and we're affecting people lives, sometimes not always for the better; the proclamation, "Churn 'em and burn 'em" must have come from somewhere. If there is a more efficient way of handling the human resource we should immediately set about to discover it – before it's too late. We need to incorporate the right level of expertise to accomplish this change. MLM leaders need to step up to the plate, make their voice and presence felt – and they need to do it now! Even small steps in the right direction will make a huge influence on a mass scale; but if we get it right, it will impact the whole industry on a colossal scale, and as my business partner Stephen Harris is constantly reminding us, if it isn't 100% right - it must be 100% wrong.

IMPORTANT NOTES

Reviews are Really Appreciated

If you have learned from this material; your feedback, support and review is vital. Please go to Amazon and leave a review - NOW: http://amzn.to/1FCM0Dv - please also pass the link to friends so that they too may enjoy Wide 'N Deep....

Thank you advance.

Go here for a FREE copy of Turbo Success. – this book will turn your life around – guaranteed! This will get also get you on our Mailing List.
Get your FREE copy here: www.TurboSuccess.com
And never look back…

Wide 'N Deep series available on KINDLE

Wide 'N Deep series available in PAPERBACK, soon: Amazon.com Barnes & Noble Lulu.com

Wide 'N Deep available on AUDIO, soon: **www.audible.com**

Contact Details for the Wizard of Kerching

Ron G Holland: Email topbizguru@hotmail.com www.RonGHolland.com

The Amazing Hersky - Stephen Harris

Email: tahersky@hotmail.com

What Follows Next is a Special FREE Bonus for You
The first chapter of my international best seller,

Turbo Success - enjoy!

Turbo Success

How to Reprogram the Human Biocomputer

Ron G Holland

Author of the international bestsellers:
Talk & Grow Rich and **Millionaire Secrets**

© Ron G Holland 1993
© Ron G Holland 2012
© Ron G Holland 2015

**THIS BOOK IS DEDICATED TO THE
MEMORY OF HOWARD HUGHES**

'When applicable, reference to the male gender implies also to the female gender and vice versa.'

Foreword

Having been an entrepreneur since the age of fourteen I have had the privilege to come under the wing of a number of mentors – various wizards who have taught me the entrepreneurial skills of selling, marketing, persistence, courage, motivation and many other things that give one the character to enable one to do whatever it is that one does.

One mentor that I want to talk about was an affable, grey haired Irishman by the name of Seamus O'Rourke, who taught me much of what I know. The old boy had the gift of the gab and I'm sure he'd kissed the Blarney Stone. He had a wonderfully colorful way in which he used the English language. He told me over and over again that we are all ordinary people, but our mission is to do extraordinary things. "Life is a do-it-yourself project, and by golly, most people are really doing it to themselves!" he'd say. Seamus told me I could do whatever it was that I wanted to do. He told me we all had the power within us to reach incredible heights way beyond our wildest possible dreams. He'd say, "If not you, who? If not now, when?"

I know you have been searching for a success formula, and for a number of years you've probably been doing it to yourself. I'd like to throw out a challenge to you. I have presented to you a success philosophy that is the most powerful human development program in the world today. Bar none! It can take you beyond your wildest possible dreams. However, you must start using it! Reading alone will not be enough. This is an instruction manual for your neck-top computer! You will have to carry out the instructions to the letter, in action as well as in spirit. Will you begin to reprogram your biocomputer for success and start to accomplish for you and yours? If not you, who? If not now, when?

Ron G Holland
London – New York – Los Angeles

CHAPTER ONE

Two Types of Success

As a young entrepreneur I used to sit on the top of "my hill" pondering over the secrets of success. I didn't have any money, but I was desperate to make some and make myself a name and a place in the world. Over a period of many years, I did make some money and I lost some money too. I always used to come back to "my hill" where I used to ponder, reflect and meditate. I always cogitated on the same question. Why is it that some people attain success very easily and others, no matter how hard they try, never accomplish their goals? After much meditation and research, as well as being a full time businessman actually working in the entrepreneurial field, many things were revealed to me. What I wanted to know about was success. I considered that I knew everything there was to know about failure! The discoveries that I made were nothing short of phenomenal and over the next few pages I will explain them all in detail. My first major discovery was that there are two types of success. The first type of success is what I would call intuitive success. I have come to the conclusion that a great many people have become eminently successful, intuitively. These people include sales people, politicians, actors, actresses, entrepreneurs and many others who have attained fabulous success, wealth and recognition and are from all walks of life. They don't really know what it is that they do to become successful and sustain that success. They just carryon doing whatever it is that they do and they become more successful. They go from success to success intuitively. Everything they touch seems to turn to gold. The second type of success is what I would call conscious success. This type of success is for people like you and me, who have seen with their own eyes the abundance the world has to offer and would very much like to participate in some of the spoils. It just so happens, that to us, all the goodies always seem just out of reach, for ourselves, at least! We know what we want and we try hard to improve. We look toward self-help books, and we try to find a success formula that will work for us and help propel us onward and upward. We search for an action plan that will work. We keep trying different approaches, we keep buying self-help books, and we never give up. Sometimes we gain a little ground! This is conscious success! And hard work it is too!

After over twenty years research into the human mind, particularly the teleological aspect (goal seeking) and research into high performance human behavior, as well as being a full time businessman, one thing became very obvious to me. This became obvious to me because I was in the field of making money and attaining success. What became obvious to me, may not have become obvious to someone who may have been studying the brain with, say, some other motive in mind. Someone who has been researching the brain with a view to finding the cure to an illness, or some other research may not have come up with the same conclusions that I have come up with. My total research has been geared up to one thing. One thing only. How we can best use our minds to accomplish success, make money, achieve happiness and reach our goals in the shortest space of time. These things I wanted to know! I spent over twenty years going into every aspect of the mind that would help me understand its innermost secrets. I made some remarkable discoveries. The common denominator of all who achieve success intuitively is that they relax and visualize the future as they desire it. If you want to attain success consciously I suggest the sooner you practice relaxing and visualizing the future as you desire it, the sooner you too will attain success. Michelangelo thought three dimensionally before he started to chip away at a piece of marble that he would produce a beautiful sculpture out of. Edward G. Robinson bought postcards of old masters and visualized exactly where he would hang them, before he actually owned them. Charlene Tilton, who played Lucy in Dallas, visualized getting the part for the job. Conrad Hilton used to play at hotels as a young boy, years before he became a hotelier. All my heroes, who I love talking about, Getty, Howard Hughes, Onassis, Edison and Winston Churchill all used to take time out to relax and visualize the future as they desired it. I can't stress this point too heavily. This is the golden thread that runs delicately through this whole work-book. J. Paul Getty wrote a number of books and articles on making money. Those books were down to earth guides to help executives in business. Getty always maintained that there were no secrets to success or magical incantations to be uttered. Getty puts his philosophy down to hard work and good executive decisions. What I say is many people become successful intuitively and have found the faculty of being able to visualize, very clearly, the future as they desire it. Something must have prompted Getty to entitle his autobiography, 'As I See It'.

Many of my students, who have completed my biocomputer seminars, have actually astonished themselves with the results they have attained. By persistently visualizing the future in a relaxed mode, many of them have attained goals, they at one time, thought impossible to reach. I too am amazed by some of the things that I have attained for myself through the constant and persistent use of relaxation and visualization. Before I walked on red hot coals on the Ray Martin Midday Show (while I was on tour in Australia) I visualized myself doing it. I also saw in my imagination, Ray Martin doing the walk with me, which he did. (That was marvelous publicity; we jammed the switchboards for over three hours!) I also visualized talking in front of a massive Amway audience and getting a standing ovation for my one hour biocomputer presentation. These, among many other things have happened to me. I wouldn't dream of doing a TV or radio interview without visualizing the complete thing in advance. I always visualize business transactions, in full in my imagination before I enter into any agreements or contracts. The results speak for themselves! I have products selling in over thirty countries around the world, and it's all come out of a vision that I've had. By relaxing and visualizing the things that I wanted to happen in the future, I have accomplished many things. I have absolute proof of how and why the technique works. I have absolute proof that every time I fail to use the technique, failure is inevitable. I know that if I keep up with the practice of relaxing and visualizing the future as I desire it, I will accomplish a lot more. I also know that if you make the start and persist with the practice, you too, will attain your wildest possible dreams. You will literally dream yourself to riches! I know the secret of success is to relax and visualize the future as you desire it. I imagine you will take a little more convincing, before you start in earnest. The following chapters are the background and the proof of how and why it works. Biocomputer seminars are fun. They're designed to be. During the course of the weekend we have many coffee breaks to allow our batteries to recharge. During the course of the weekend everyone gets a chance to stand up and say his or her piece. That piece is to help gel and integrate the learning process. Over the years I have learnt more from my biocomputer students than I could ever hope to teach them. I hope you pick up a few pointers too. All the time be looking to see if any of their comments apply to you. Before we start a biocomputer seminar I ask my students what they want out of the weekend. It's interesting to see how they develop over the weekend, their skepticism falls away, their confidence rises, as a whole new world unfolds!

LIVE AT THE BIOCOMPUTER SEMINAR:

USA: Darlene, "I know exactly what I want out of this weekend. All my life I only ever get so far. I keep reaching plateaus. I never get ahead. I want to live an exciting lifestyle."

USA: Frederick, "I have a business that's in trouble. A friend told me to come here, he said it would change my life."

Ireland: Geoff, "I'm in the Multi-Level Marketing business. I know lots of people who have made a lot of money. I want to join them."

Australia: Helen, "I want my business to succeed; I'm hanging in there at the moment, but only just."

USA: Bud, "I go to all the seminars; I heard this was a good one, that's why I'm here."

Poland: Andrew, "I want to understand more about the mind. I read 'Talk & Grow Rich' and I wanted to hear you speak."

Singapore: Madalyn, "I'm in an industry that is very tough and competitive. I need some tools to get me ahead of the competition."

USA: Nat, "I want to be a millionaire. I've come close on a number of occasions but I've always gone bust."

USA: Jack, "I've built up so many businesses, but I must have a business destruct mode that I go into. I recognize it' but I just don't seem able to do anything about it."

USA: Ron, "I've only got one goal - everything!"

USA: Ross, "I want to be a successful career woman. I'm prepared to pay the price. I've read a lot and do a lot of seminars and workshops. Nothing really works for me except hard work."

Australia: Manfred, "I want my own plane and my own business. I can fly, it's my passion, but without a plane it's not much fun."

Australia: Polly, "I just want lots of fun. I want lots of money too!"

Australia: Malcolm, "I'm in the insurance industry and I don't get enough appointments."

USA: Marion, "I want to be happily married. I was abused as a child and I think that's screwing up my relationships."

Ireland: Sam, "I run my own company but it's like I'm on a treadmill. Stop the world and let me get off!" England: Graham, "I read your book, I wanted to hear more of the same."

England: Sue, "I'm with him!"

USA: Roger, "I've got to do something different. I've had the same goals for over ten years and I haven't accomplished any of them."

USA: Allen, "I'm already successful but I want to go even higher.",

USA: Freda, "I'm stuck in my career and I want to get out and move into the big money in another career, I just don't know how. I'm hoping you can tell me."

Singapore: Ng, "If I keep doing what I keep doing I'll end up going broke. I can't get motivated."

USA: Heath, "Last week two of my colleagues came here, I have never seen such a dramatic change in two people, ever."

USA: Wes, "I have one goal, I want a friend."

USA: Erick, "I want to get my invention manufactured and into the world market place. Once I've done that I'll be a millionaire."

USA: Fred, "I wanna be a millionaire!"

USA: Max, "I have a burning desire to be a Diamond in the Amway business and live the life style of a millionaire. Then I want to be a Double Diamond."

England: Karen, "I already have my own successful business but I want more security. It doesn't feel right at the moment."

Poland: Marek, "It wouldn't make sense going through life not knowing what my real potential was."

Spain: Michael, "Your reputation preceded you. You come highly recommended. My wife and I are looking forward to the weekend immensely."

England: Patrick, "I'm a seminar junkie. I buy all the books and tapes. Nothing has ever worked, I wish it would."

ZOOM SECRETS!

1. Recognize that many of the things that you may have done successfully in the past may have been intuitive.
2. Many people who have become successful intuitively have failed and never reached great heights again, because they didn't know exactly what they did to get there in the first place.
3. Realize that you have fantastic control over your life and your environment, because you actually and factually know the secret of conscious success.
4. It helps tremendously if we really do know what creates successful outcomes rather than use hit-and-miss methods.
5. You know that conscious success depends on relaxing, and visualizing the future as you desire it.

ADDENDUM

ISN'T THAT PYRAMID SELLING?

A VERY POSITIVE BOOK ABOUT NETWORK MARKETING!

Ron G Holland
Author of international bestsellers *Talk & Grow Rich*
and *Millionaire Secrets*

© 2009 - 2015 Ron G Holland

Contents

What exactly is Pyramid selling?
So what's Network Marketing?
Network Marketing v Pyramid Selling - how to tell the good from the bad
Network Marketing - the business opportunity of the Millennium
Remuneration and Rewards
    Unilevel
    Stair Step-Breakaway
    Matrix
    Binary
    Hybrid
    Two-up
Working Out the Best Plan for You
The advantages of Network Marketing
Dreams, Goals, Aspirations....and a Desire to Make Money
Thousands are quietly making a small fortune
Word of mouth advertising
What do big corporations, governments, the military and religious organisations have in common?
Why is network marketing so powerful?
Recruiting
Training
Cost Effective Marketing
Exponential or Geometric Growth
A Business of your Own, but not on Your Own
Rules, Regulations and Fair Trading
How to tell a genuine opportunity from a scam

What next?

What exactly is Pyramid selling?

Pyramid selling is illegal. It is based on the concept that someone buys product (or service, ie. a club membership) at a price, adds a profit margin and sells to the next third person and so on, until the product becomes too expensive to sell and it ends up in someone's garage. Many times there is not even a product involved, the scheme simply revolves around people passing money to each other (a money-go-round) and relies totally on more and more people entering the scheme. So in reality, this scheme is NOT workable. Here's why. E.G: The type of product is irrelevant but for the sake of this example let's look at 1000 tins of aerosol paint which have a usual retail price of $1. These would be sold to the first "level" for, say 50cents. The first level purchaser is then required to find someone else to buy the consignment for, say 60cents or even 70cents. Clearly after one or two trading manoeuvres the product becomes too expensive to buy in a consignment - no one will buy 1000 cans at $1 when they can buy them individually at the local shop. At each level, part of the profit is passed upwards to the level above until "the last man in the chain" gets stuck with product he cannot sell and he loses his money. This loss of money by the "last man" is inevitable from the commencement of the scheme, and as such, the system is easily identifiable as a "con" trick.

So what is Network Marketing?

Network Marketing (sometimes called a trading scheme, Multi-level marketing (MLM) or referral marketing) is totally different. In this case no-one ends up with a quantity of useless product in their basement or garage. Everyone buys product from the company that they use personally as well as sell to others. What's more, they only buy the amount of product that they can use/sell in a reasonable period and often only when they have a customer to buy it. They then replace their stock, as and when they need it. Following the example above, where aerosol cans of paint are the product, the following Network Marketing scenario is totally different. e.g. The first difference would be the number of cans bought. Usually there is no minimum. Each can has a pre-set wholesale price, say 70cents, and a recommended retail price say $1. Any member participating in the Network Marketing business can buy as much or as little stock as he/she needs at wholesale price. The idea then is to sell it at retail price and make a profit. Another major difference is that most participants usually find their customers before placing their order for product from the company. The final difference is that in network marketing most companies also operate a stock buy back policy in the event that any participant wants to leave the scheme.

Network Marketing v Pyramid Selling - how to tell the good from the scams

Network Marketing
1. Minimal investment required
2. Legal buy back arrangements
3. No income generated from enrolments
4. Self promotion is a major plus
5. Fixed buying & selling prices

Pyramid Selling
1. A large investment is usually needed to 'join'
2. Distributors can be caught with large amounts of unwanted stock
3. Major income is generated from enrolments
4. Self promotion is virtually non-existent
5. Prices are set according to your position in the chain

Genuine Network Marketing - the business opportunity of the Millennium

Network Marketing is a highly ethical and practical business that is currently responsible for creating **sales well in excess of $16 billion dollars annually.** Successful companies have a product or a service (or both) that is sold outside the network. In many instances companies follow the U.S. legal guidelines, which require **over 70%** of the product to be sold, or personally consumed, before more product can be purchased. This is good business practice.

Furthermore, no-one in the network earns any money at all, unless product is sold. Once product is sold, however, the profit on that product is distributed to the Networkers according to the marketing plan. Networking is predominately a "people" industry in which distributors of products can earn impressive rewards for recruiting, teaching, training and motivating others to sell products and become successful.

Remuneration and Rewards
There are many different ways of making money in Network Marketing (network reward plans). Here are the six most common:

1. Unilevel
A simple plan, with unlimited width, so that the frontline can have as many people enrolled in it as you like, and a limited depth. Most Unilevel plans pay out to a depth of five levels but seven and eight are not uncommon. Many have compression to help address the limited depth payout and any fall out.

2. Stair Step-Breakaway
This is presently the most common compensation plan. The plan has two sides, the front ("stair-step") and the back (breakaway"). The front side has increasing rank positions

that are achieved by meeting specified volume requirements in your group until your personal volume is at a level where you and your group breakaway. Usually breakaway plans allow unlimited width, ie. you can sponsor as many people as you like on your front line. Many of these plans have quotas and group volume requirements in order to qualify for bonuses. Most pay six levels deep, but they have been known to pay nine levels deep. Most compress volume up, so that non-active distributors don't get commission and the active ones will pick up the rewards. Override commissions are based on both personal volume and personal group sales.

3. Matrix

With a fixed matrix you can usually sponsor only a fixed number of people on your front line. If you sponsor more, - and you are actively encouraged to do so – then those extra distributors "spillover" into the levels below, so down lines grow much faster. Usually matrix are six wide and six deep, or two wide and twelve deep. This type of plan lends itself admirably to certain service-related products like buying and service companies and subscription sales with a fixed monthly cost. An

unfixed matrix (such as the Unilevel or stair step breakaway) will allow you to sponsor unlimited people on your front line. It is important that commission in the matrix. It has been argued that "spillover" can interfere with a participants and management and training responsibilities.

4. Binary

These plans are becoming increasingly popular. A binary plan is a fixed matrix with two wide on the front line. There are many ways in which binary plans operate, however; most of the binary plans coming out of the USA, have no limit on levels and distributors are paid on the volume in the group, usually weekly. To make the most money you have to balance the two legs or sides in your organisation. If not, you will be paid out on the weak leg and the surplus money you are due on the strong leg will be held in "escrow" until you do manage to balance the legs. Participants may have business centres or income centres, rather than one fixed position in the network, and many hold a number of positions in their down lines.

5. Hybrid

This plan is simply a combination of other plans, ie. they take various components from a number of plans in an endeavour to create an even more effective marketing programme. Hybrid plans started in the United States when a number of party plan operators found it beneficial to motivate their party planners to recruit as well as sell. This may not be a bad way to go, bearing in mind all plans have their "pros" and "cons." but it can become complex and hence difficult to explain to participants.

6. Two-up

The two up plan works by you giving your first two recruits to your up line sponsor. After that, the first two recruits they sponsor go to you and at that point you start earning commission. Lots of these plans have started, then failed. In fact, right now I cannot think of a single one that has succeeded. They also generally have a bad reputation.

Working Out the Best Plan for You

All plans have their pros and cons. So, by all means look at the marketing plan, but also look beyond. Look at the products and services, the people who are already involved, the marketing literature, the Code of Ethics, the atmosphere at Business Opportunity Meetings, the training that is available, the sales and marketing tools supplied by the company.

The advantages of Network Marketing

- a business of your own
- virtually no overheads
- flexible working hours
- extensive travel - often global
- a chance to build a business to any size you desire maybe even bigger than the person who introduced you to the opportunity in the first place.
- a real chance of financial independence if you work hard
- time with your family - they can work and travel with you.
- you are building a business of your own, but not on your own.

Dreams, Goals, Aspirations and a Burning Desire to Make Money

Most people have dreams, goals, aspirations and a burning desire to make money. What they don't have is a vehicle. They don't have a product or service, a marketing method that works, or a reward system. Network marketing offers all of these and much more. Indeed, for many people it's the perfect business opportunity. For several reasons. It has a low level entry fee, it's low risk, you work when and where you want to, it's an exciting "people" business, with travel, new friends and associates and - once you've built a network - an extremely healthy cash flow. Indeed, networking offers everyone the chance to earn a very serious income, maybe a fortune, if they work hard and motivate their group to do the same. What's more, network marketing offers the same opportunity to everybody.

"Twenty years from now you will be more disappointed by the things that you didn't do than by the ones you did do. So throw off the bowlines. Sail away from safe harbour. Catch the trade winds in your sail. Explore. Dream. Discover." - *Mark Twain*

Whereas once Network Marketing was heavily biased towards housewives and those between jobs, today it is recognised as one of the key areas of growth for the new millennium. This fact alone has changed the demographics of network marketing beyond recognition. Already there are literally tens of thousands of professionals involved in network marketing. Doctors, lawyers, accountants, dentists, real estate people, actors, brokers, teachers, insurance salesmen. All quietly building networks and making money, in addition to their already substantial salaries. They see Network Marketing as the key to their future security and happily, while they're building their network nest-egg, the flexible working hours fit in seamlessly with their already hectic schedules.

Thousands are quietly making a small fortune and others are making LARGE fortunes...

Network Marketing is predominantly a word-of-mouth business with people talking to each other and "sharing" their products and services. Most Networkers never need to advertise to sell their products or services, they just network! One US-based Network company alone turns over $7 billion a year and has been trading successfully for over forty years. That company advertises a little, but most don't. In fact, networking is the world's best kept secret, with millions of people all quietly beavering away on their way to a potential fortune. Some, of course, only earn an extra $50 or $100 a week - and that suits them fine. However, for the more ambitious Networker there is the opportunity to become very successful.

Word of mouth advertising – referral marketing

Networking works through people getting out into the world and referring companies rely on their participants to get out there and refer their products to other people. You have been doing this for years and not getting paid for it.

Take the example of a good book that you have read, you'll recommend it to maybe four or five people. The same as a good movie, show or nice restaurant. You recommend that product or service to friends. Networking companies do the same thing, except they reward you for recommending their product. The primary reason why Network Marketing companies can pass so much money back to their distributors is the very fact that they do not spend millions of pounds on advertising and distribution. The distributors fulfil the role of promoting the product (via word of mouth advertising, i.e. recommending the products to friends, relatives and others in their sphere of influence. This includes their warm market and others whom they come into contact with on a day-to-day basis), and they also take on the roles of distributing those products. The money otherwise allocated to these two costly overhead items is what is used to pay the distributors. The commission that distributors receive is commonly referred to as a "word of mouth advertising bonus."

What do big corporations, governments, the military and religious organisations have in common?

The one thing that the Vatican, Pentagon, White House and large corporations all have in common is the type of structure that would appear to have a figurehead at the top, who work closely with maybe five or six key people, and below that, each one of those key people work with five or six key people of their own. It has been said that Jesus was the best Networker of all time. He had a front line of only twelve, but they spread the word, and still are spreading the word of Christianity to millions.

Why is network marketing so powerful?

Network marketing is so powerful because a number of things are accomplished so very simply and at the same time effectively.

1 Recruiting

In a conventional Direct Sales force the sales manager has to recruit his team. He then has to go about training them and also motivating them. This is usually highly inefficient and ineffective and usually the sales manager ends up spreading himself too thin. In MLM everyone has the chance to recruit new members or participants.

2 Training

Again in direct selling the sales manager has to train his team. There is only so much he can do and at the end of the day even if he trains them all brilliantly, unfortunately that's where the dissemination of knowledge ends. In networking you are responsible for training the people in your down line. This is one of the major reasons why you can earn so much money for training and motivating the people below you.

3 Cost Effective Marketing

Because everyone in the network has a chance to earn substantial income for effective work at little or no risk, the whole team is motivated to achieve, sell products and recruit people.

4 Exponential or Geometric Growth

This one factor alone is responsible for making people millions and it's how you can make a fortune too. Because you "recruit two" who "recruit two" each, taking advantage of exponential growth, a substantial network builds very quickly, and you have a chance to earn on the products sold by people in your group. A lot of money, especially if you have trained and motivated them well.

A Business of your Own, but not on Your Own

When you get involved in a Network Marketing company you are building your own business. Treat it like your own business and treat it as a big business, for that is exactly what it is. The good thing about networking is that there is always plenty of help and training available from others who wish you to succeed.

Rules, Regulations and Fair Trading (UK)

There are many laws and guidelines to protect consumers who wish to reap the rewards of Network Marketing. These laws include, but are not limited to, Trading Schemes Regulations 1997, Trading Schemes Act 1996, Prices Act 1974, Sale of Goods Act 1979, Fair Trading Act 1973. In the UK, the industry trade association for Network Marketing companies is the Direct Selling Association (DSA). This body has its own Codes and monitors its member Network Marketing companies to ensure they stick to both the law and the Codes. The DSA also runs a membership scheme so that legitimate companies can show that they are approved. Membership is not automatic, it is something for a new company to strive for. When achieved, members must display the DSA logo on all their paperwork, contracts etc.

How to tell a genuine opportunity from a scam

One of the real keys to looking out for a genuine opportunity is that it will have products and services that can be sold week after week without any problem. Beware of an opportunity that requires you to persuade others to join if you cannot see tangible proof of what the money is for. The criteria which identify a respectable network marketing company are easy to identify.

1. Is there a genuine product or service?
2. Are there genuine customers, not just participants finding new participants on a "money-go-round"?
3. Is the pricing and commission structure fixed and published?
4. Are the Direct Selling Association's Rules being followed, even if the company is not a formal member of the DSA?
5. Is the company a member of the DSA, or is membership a realistic possibility? (Remember this is not automatic. Perfectly legitimate NM businesses are working towards DSA membership. Not being a member does not necessarily indicate any flaw in the company.)

What next?

For those who wish to study the detail of the law, Appendices 1-3 provide a comprehensive overview of the subject and include five sections from a major law firm, which are, of course, reproduced with their kind permission.

Appendix 1

The Trading Schemes Act 1996. (UK)

The main intention of the Trading Schemes Act is to prohibit schemes which offer substantial rewards to members for doing no more than recruiting others. To catch as many businesses in the definition as possible, there are now just two criteria to fulfil:

The participants in the scheme expect to receive financial benefits from any or all of the following:

- Introducing others to the scheme
- Promoting others within the scheme
- Supplying goods or services to any person
- The acquisition of goods or services by any person

Goods or Services or both provided by the person promoting the scheme are either:

- To be supplied by the participants (whether as participant for the promoter or otherwise) to other persons; or
- To be supplied by the promoter to persons introduced by participants. Clearly, this covers all genuine Network Marketing organisations. Once again the importance of the supply of goods and/or services is emphasised and is evident in both sections of the new definition. It bears repeating that this is usually the best indicator of a

legitimate operation. However, the new definition is much more satisfactory than the old one.

The Scam Operations should easily fall under the rules and can then be prosecuted if they do not comply with them. Pyramids fall under the rules. (Chain letters were excluded from the regulations because the DTI already regarded them as illegal under the Lotteries Act).

Appendix 2

The Trading schemes Regulations 1997. (UK)

The Regulations contain detailed explanations as to how a legitimate Network Marketing business must be run. Some of the most important points are included below.

• In the first 7 days of participation a new participant must not pay or agree to pay more than £200 (in the UK) to the company.

• In the first 14 days of participation a new participant is entitled to all of their money back and they may return any goods they have bought without paying any handling charges for doing so.

• A participant has buy-back rights which can be exercised on leaving the scheme

• The content of advertisements for the scheme is controlled. They must include the following warning:

Statutory Information:
i) It is illegal for a promoter or a participant in a trading scheme to persuade anyone to make a payment by promising benefits from others to join a trading scheme
ii) Do not be misled by claims that high earnings are easily achieved. The content of contracts for the scheme is controlled. In addition to the above they must include the following:
iii) If you sign this contract you have 14 days in which to cancel and get your money back.

Other matters covered by the regulations include:
- Pre-performance by the promoter
- Securities and guarantees
- Record keeping
- Recovery of commission on termination
- Civil consequences of contravention of the Regulations

Appendix 3

What the professionals look for
The following 5 sections are reproduced by kind permission of our Lawyers, a major city law firm.

Pyramid scheme not defined in legislation.
1. The Fair Trading Act defines a "trading scheme" and then regulates (primarily through the Trading Schemes Regulations 1997) how those schemes should operate. However, a scheme which breaches

a provision in the Trading Schemes Regulations is not necessarily an unlawful scheme or a pyramid scheme simply because of that breach. Conversely, a scheme may comply with the Trading Schemes Regulations yet still be declared unlawful by the Courts. Although a "pyramid scheme" is not defined in the legislation, the type of scheme at which the Fair Trading Act is aimed was summarised in the Official Report of the House of Commons, namely: "Get-rich-quick schemes operating on the same basis as chain letters with each member recruiting further members. Members pay out large sums in the expectation of a high return. These payments are nearly always based on unrealistic forecasts of earnings from recruitment. These forecasts are derived from the principle of geometric progression, leading to theoretical levels of recruitment reward which, in reality, are impossible to achieve."

Unlawful schemes, lotteries or against the public interest.
2. There is a difficulty in categorically stating that any particular scheme is lawful based on a review of its scheme documentation alone, as it is quite possible for the documentation used for a scheme to comply with all of the relevant regulations yet for the scheme itself to be unlawful. The main reason for this is that whilst the laws governing the scheme documents are relatively clear and can usually be

complied with simply by "desk top" drafting (provided that the promoter then complies in practice with the terms of its own documents), the Fair Trading Act does not define categories of lawful or unlawful schemes; rather, it creates a couple of important specific offences and then regulates schemes which fall within its definition of a "trading scheme". It is then left to the Courts to determine whether a particular trading scheme is unlawful, relying in the main either upon the scheme being against the "public interest", which may be because it is "inherently objectionable as being ultimately bound to fail", or because it is a "lottery", in addition to the specific "recruitment payments" offence under Section 120 (3) of the Fair Trading Act.

Money circulation schemes, chain letters and unlawful lotteries.

3. In the past schemes have been declared unlawful, for example, because they have no goods or services (such as the obvious "money circulation" or "chain letter" schemes), or because although it has goods and services the rewards which a participant in truth will receive are derived from orders placed by other participants and not from sales to end-users achieved by that participant. The Courts treat the latter such schemes as "lotteries" within the meaning of the Lotteries Act 1976, on the basis that because the

rewards to be obtained by a participant result from orders given by persons over whom that participant has no control then such rewards depend, so far as he is concerned, not upon his skill or work but upon pure chance, and hence the scheme is a "lottery".

Why the participant is described as having no control over the orders placed.

4. Because the goods are not "genuine" goods which the participant has the ability to sell on their own merits he must rely upon other persons placing orders because they are motivated by a desire to participate in the scheme. In such cases the goods have been described as "a peg on which the lottery is hung" (Global Pioneers case 1984). So, for example, in the leading case of D.P.P. v Phillips (1934) the promoter bought a supply of notecases at less than 10 pence each and signed up distributors who had to buy a notecase for £1 and obtain orders for notecases from customers also for £1. The distributor earned no commission on the first three sales but thereafter qualified for a commission of 50 cents on each $1 notecase sold by the promoter on orders obtained by the distributor or his downline. The Court held that the scheme was an unlawful lottery as - with the exception of commission resulting from orders directly obtained by the distributor himself - all the commissions which he received were from orders given by persons over

whom he had no control and would depend, so far as he was concerned, not upon his skill or work but upon pure chance. In the Phillips case Lord Hewart said "The Court has to disengage, if it can, the reality of the transaction from the appearance which for obvious reasons it is made to assume. In my opinion this was not a commercial transaction. The object of the seller and the object of the buyer were not concerned with notecases. They were concerned with the chance which the buyer might procure of obtaining a large sum of money by the operation of persons over whom he had no more control than he has over the countless laughter of the sea, which does not laugh when the sun is not shining." Similarly, in the "Titan Business Club" (July 1996) the Court held that the scheme (which in its original form at the time of this Court Judgement involved no products or services but consisted entirely of the sale of participations in itself, with distributors receiving commissions from the membership fees paid by new members introduced by them") was an unlawful lottery. The Court approved the Phillips decision: Lord Justice Saville said "an over-analytical approach should not be adopted, but rather one of common sense. In the present case, the reality of the matter is undoubtedly that those persuaded to join the scheme did so and paid their money in the hope of the rewards that would result from those afterwards joining their particular "family tree"."

Misleading advertisements.

5 The Control of Misleading Advertisements Regulations 1988 give powers to the Office of Fair Trading to apply to Court for an injunction against any person appearing to be concerned with the publication of a misleading advertisement, and the Office of Fair Trading is most likely to take such action when a publisher has failed to respond to a complaint or finding by the ASA that the advertisement is in breach of its Codes. The essential concern of the Advertising Code is with the content of advertisements, applying the general principle that advertisement should be "legal, decent, honest and truthful". It does not presume to judge whether what is being advertised is worth buying, nor does it act as censor on matters of taste.

The current situation

The 1973 Act allows the Secretary of State to create regulations governing the industry. The Act has recently been amended and what follows is a brief resume of the current position. Due to the difficulties experienced with the 1973 four part definition of a trading scheme, it was decided to broaden the new definition in order to catch as many schemes as possible, then create new regulations to control them. What is now the Trading Schemes Act 1996 was originally introduced to Parliament as a private members" bill by Sir Nicholas Scott with the support of the Direct Selling Association (DSA) which is the industry watchdog. The Trading Schemes Act 1996 was passed and it was hoped that this would create a workable system of regulation for the legitimate businesses, while expunging the current fraudsters and dissuading any prospective ones from starting up. The Direct selling industry was then worth about £1bn in retail trade and the Government recognised that it provided many people with an excellent opportunity for part time earnings. The Trading Schemes Act 1996 replaced Section 118 of The Fair Trading Act 1973 with a two part definition for trading schemes. This was much wider than the previous definition and its purpose was to catch all versions of Network Marketing types of business. New regulations were then issued to make the businesses which now come under the Act comply with strict but fair criteria. This was to ensure that the public are protected, the scams are out of business and probably most important, the legitimate Network Marketing businesses can show that they are reputable and safe for the public to invest both their time and money in. The new regulations are called The Trading Schemes Regulations 1997. They became law on 6th February 1997. They replaced the old "Pyramid Selling Regulations 1989"

A MESSAGE FROM RON G HOLLAND

WHAT TO DO NEXT?

WHAT ELSE CAN I DO FOR YOU? – LOTS, BELIEVE ME!
I help create Millionaires – and have been doing so for the past thirty years! Will you be my next success story?

I hope you enjoyed reading and listening to Wide 'N Deep as much as I enjoyed writing and narrating it. I can help you more than you know and I would ask you to not only read the following paragraphs, but study them and then take appropriate action.

HELP YOURSELF - TELL THREE FRIENDS ABOUT THE WIDE 'N DEEP – MULTI LEVEL MAGIC SERIES
Yes, this is a way of me making more sales – for sure. But there's more. I think it is crucial that you get yourself together small mastermind group to start brainstorming these ideas with. If you have a group and you're all on the same page you will grow together and it is highly likely you'll give each good feedback, keep each other motivated and help each other solve problems.

HOW A REVIEW WILL HELP BOTH OF US

Obviously the more reviews I get the more books I sell and the more I get motivated to write and produce great stuff, (even if some of the books do take four years to write) that will propel you onward and upward. I believe there is loads of stuff; mentoring, fund raising, advice, introductions, who knows what else, that we could do together and one day, perhaps in the very near future we're going to meet; on email, Skype, or face-to-face at one of my global events.

RON G HOLLAND MENTORING – WILL YOU BE MY NEXT SUCCESS STORY?

I still have the capacity to take on a limited number of clients who I will personally help take to the next level. To qualify, your business needs to be at least three years old and turning over a minimum of $500,000 a year. The mentoring program is an extremely rigorous, robust and clever process based on business acumen and mind power techniques that I have developed over thirty year period; and is predominantly based on video skype and email. I have a track record in helping entrepreneurs become millionaires. I am particularly keen to talk to business owners turning over more than $10,000,000 but may have plateaued, but still have a burning desire to go to $100,000,000 and beyond. Email me at: TopBizGuru@hotmail.com and tell me briefly about your business, including your website, and I will then come back to you quickly and tell you in detail about my services and how we may move forward. I look forward hearing from you.

Over a thirty-year period ron has helped create numerous millionaires and received thousands of testimonials, here's a handful...

Ron is one of the world's leading exponents on the subject of thinking and non-thinking and he has given numerous business seminars and presentations and has been interviewed on TV, radio, Podcasts and press across four continents.

Written up as: 'Leading Motivational Speaker', 'Jedi Master of Wealth Creation', The Juggernaut, 'Top Biz Guru', 'Entrepreneur's Entrepreneur'. and, 'The incredible Ron G Holland, quite possibly the very greatest business and self-development guru...Fleet Street Publications.

I am 48 years old and I picked up a copy of Talk & Grow Rich approximately 25 years ago when I was a green salesman selling copiers for Canon. I read the book over and over and took it everywhere I went (like a Talisman). I went into the business with an associate and have built up a successful company and become a multimillionaire. It has not been easy and we made big mistakes and got ripped off a few times but I still remember so many of your principles and I'm truly thankful for the advice! Much Respect! **Rob Kedgley**

Ron held my hand until I got the first million in the bank and I am now a multi-millionaire with international homes around the world. **Andy Hunt**

Without question of a doubt Ron Holland's Talk & Grow Rich helped become millionaire. I am Ron's greatest fan and now he is my personal mentor. **Robert Frater**

Ron saved me from Bankruptcy – TWICE!
Harry Roberts

Ron Holland slashed our marketing costs by 50% and improved our closure rate by 30%. Incredible!
 Neil Murphy

The investors that Ron introduced me to so far have invested over $750,000 into my business. Not bad for a 25 year old. **Mike Jones.**

Ron helped us raise over $2,000,000 when everyone had failed to do so. **Michael Kraftman.**

Be in no doubt of Ron Holland's work ethic, ability to cut through jargon while stimulating that bio-supercomputer, will leave you amazed. He has black book to die for! I can recommend him most highly and I am privileged to have worked with him and allowed his rare breed of magic to rub off a little in my direction. I am very grateful indeed.
Tim Dingle - BSc (Hons) PGCE MBA

IMPORTANT NOTES

Reviews are Really Appreciated

If you have learned from this material; your feedback, support and review is vital. Please go to Amazon and leave a review - NOW: http://amzn.to/1FCM0Dv - please also pass the link to friends so that they too may enjoy the Wide 'N Deep series…thank you advance.

Grab a FREE copy of Turbo Success – This book will turn your life around – guaranteed! This action get also get you on our Mailing List.
www.TurboSuccess.com

And never look back…

The Wide 'N Deep series is available: on Kindle and Paperback at Amazon and Audio at Audible and iTunes

OUR CONTACT DETAILS

The Wizard of Kerching - Ron G Holland

Email: **TopBizGuru@hotmail.com**

www.RonGHolland.com

The Amazing Hersky - Stephen Harris:

Email: **tahersky@hotmail.com**

ACTION PLAN

Printed in Great Britain
by Amazon